THE LIBERATED ZONE

THE LIBERATED ZONE

A
GUIDE
TO
CHRISTIAN
RESISTANCE

John
Pairman
Brown

SCM PRESS LTD
LONDON

Biblical quotations are from the Revised Standard
Version of the Bible copyright in 1946 and 1952

334 00892 1

First British edition 1970
published by SCM Press Ltd
56 Bloomsbury Street London WC1B 3QX

© John Pairman Brown 1969

Typeset in the United States of America
Printed in Great Britain by
Lewis Reprints Ltd
Port Talbot, Glamorgan

For Chuck Jones,
who lived with the writing,
and for all his buddies.

PREFACE

The big difference Gutenberg made is that now, when a writer sees his words in the unfamiliar type of galley proof, he wants to explain about his new thing that he's done. What the reader finds in his hands is people's theology, in as close to our American tongue as I could put it. By theology I mean the most important things a man has to say—a man who stands where things are happening. And what's happening today is that people, for better or worse, are taking matters over from an Establishment into their own control, and don't propose to relinquish them.

Some theology is international, written by men in whatever tongue was convenient: Aquinas, Calvin, Tillich. We shouldn't let ourselves forget that Jesus and Paul really had no mother tongue either. Still it's easier to admire the author who expresses the aspirations of his people in its own idiom. If we ask for a more or less systematic work, conceived in the rhythms of the English language, and concerned with the actual problems of its own time, after we've said Richard Hooker in Britain and Reinhold Niebuhr in America, we hesitate before naming others. And these men give us not people's theology but official theology; they were the advisers, at one or two removes, to princes.

So I send off my book as a counter-Establishment theology, in our provincial dialect, called out by the Viet Nam war: a transposition of Hooker or Niebuhr into a minor key. This is not self-deprecating. In the history of Israel, the career of Jesus, the course of the Church, we see the apostolic succession of love flowing along the same electric cable as imperial history, but with a 90-degree difference of phase. Minor is the right thing to be. It's the unique key to wisdom, which the authorities of Mordor can take away only from those who cooperate with them.

These chapters represent the first (or background) semester of what I meant to cover with my seminarians at the Associated Theological Schools in Berkeley. Each chapter has its own history, and the whole is something of a mosaic. If there are cracks in the mortar, I hope it's because the individual squares were hard and well-cut. On pages 17-19 I outline the argument of the whole; here I record previous states of each part.

Chapter I, which traces out the contemporary crisis of violence, is a late report to Tom Hayes and the Episcopal Peace Fellowship, who helped me go round the world via Prague and Hanoi in fall of 1967—as well as to my patient SDS traveling companions. It records the failure of an expatriate at readjusting to the managed American environment; and revises downward the honor which Gibson Winter and Harvey Cox pay to the metropolis as bearer of the future. With the kind permission of Prof. F. J. Trembley of Lehigh University I've used his unpublished paper "Environmental Crises."

Chapter II summarizes the understanding of ancient history, as providing both the cause and the cure of violence, which I worked out with my students at the American University of Beirut from 1958 to 1965. Traces appear of scholarly hobbies: Phoenician culture, the common Mediterranean vocabulary, the reconstruction of the Synoptic tradition. Prof. George Field of Berkeley has helped with cosmology, and K. A. Wittfogel's *Oriental Despotism* with the meaning of irrigation-control in ancient society. I conclude with an attempt to define the importance of Jesus' innovations in strictly historical terms.

Chapter III, on revolutionary nonviolence, is the expansion of a paper done in February 1967 for the Department of Christian Social Relations in the Executive Council of the Episcopal Church. My best thanks are due to the Rev. Herschel Halbert for making me write down these views, which are not necessarily to be associated with him or the Council. The reader will have available for comparison, as I did not, the full text of James W. Douglass' *The Non-Violent Cross*.

Chapter IV refines a study of the way divine names are used which I've read at various philosophy colloquia. I propose that the linguistic analysts and the death-of-God people should sit down and read the ancient texts which are our only clue to the intended meaning of language about the Gods. They'll find, I think, that all along they've been doing the same thing as classical scholars, and that each can learn from the other. Insistence on historical method leads to an actual contemporary translation of the noun "God."

Chapter V radicalizes my essays on Church renewal and re-union which have appeared in *The Christian Century,* Malcolm Boyd's *The Underground Church,* and elsewhere. The National Council of Churches and the Consultation on Church Union are asked to recognize that the era of Constantine is finished, and that their assigned job—replacing violence by reconciliation—is actually being done by the Civil Rights Movement, the American Friends Service Committee, the National Mobilization to End the War in Vietnam, Clergy and Laymen Concerned about Vietnam, the Resistance, and the Fellowship of Reconciliation.

I have the Rev. Deaconess Esther Davis, Lynda Barbour, and my much put-upon wife to thank for a rush job of typing. At one point I had some personal possessiveness about this text; I was cured of it by my kind editors, who through. applying intelligence to the MS have liberated the argument to speak for itself. It's some kind of an augury that the work of a maverick Yankee Episcopalian can come out from an official Southern Presbyterian press.

I'm aware of having produced a mostly impersonal and ideo-logical study of historical movements. An earlier book was personal and disengaged. I'm pushing ahead now to do something which will be both personal and committed: spelling out the individual con-sistency which is the necessary interior of any social change for the better. But putting books into print is just a by-product of the main job: helping people get built together in communities where history and nature, the cathedral and the forest, will once again begin to make the same kind of sense. So a number of these observations al-ready rest on my work at the Free Church of Berkeley, with (besides many others) Tony Nugent, Glee Bishop, and Dick and Joy York, whose courage earlier made the writing of these pages possible. And if a group somewhere wants to organize itself along anything like the lines here suggested, I'll be glad to come on and consult with them up to the limits of my energy and skill.

        Berkeley
        November 2, 1968
        All Souls' and third anniversary
            of Norman Morrison's death by fire

CONTENTS

For Nature herself will be liberated
out of enslavement to corruption,
into the glorious freedom
of the sons of God.

PAUL, TO THE ROMANS 8:21*

---

* Unless otherwise indicated, Scripture quotations are the author's translations.

I

THE ESCALATION OF VIOLENCE

1. Introduction

(a) On living in occupied territory

This book is written for men and women who, like its author, woke up one morning to discover they were living in occupied territory; who see a resistance movement going on in their neighborhood and would like to make the scene.

The crisis is global, and the ulceration which has surfaced here might break out wherever human beings misuse potentially unlimited power. Still Americans have unique guilt and opportunity. And not all of them are accustomed to thinking underground.

Is this language literal or metaphorical? The New Testament raises the same problem; are its evil Principles supernatural entities or Roman imperial officials? Asking the question that way obscures the actual data— a pervasive demonic exploitation exercised through the institutions of an established State. By adopting the terminology of people's revolution I claim it as the valid political language for our time, and go back to an old tradition of using political language for a more-than-political declaration of independence.

The student hasn't enrolled in a course of lectures, but a seminar—the product of extensive discussion with both Establishment types and revolutionaries around the world. I'm not conscious here of altering the analysis in a previous book, *The Displaced Person's Almanac*, except so far as the crisis has become more acute, and our involvement deeper. The refugee and the guerrilla are intended to be passive and active symbols for the same character. As the world judges, the same man can't be both victim and revolutionary. But the new mode of living which is folly to Greeks and scandal to Jews can only be grasped by such pairs of complementary images.

The demonic powers which have infiltrated our society are entrenched in ourselves. A Christian Resistance is one on its guard against dangers from its home territory. I saw no reason not to name it after its historical origin. And so these pages are intended as a practical manual for my brothers and sisters in setting up a free Church around them.

Unlike other animals, we're learning to recognize the signs of order and disorder in nature. In our own society they are harder to identify. Only a Jägerstätter saw that something stunk in Hitler's Germany, only a Luther guessed that a Reformation was in the womb. In America of the sixties, the mass media have trained us to expect that if something is decaying or coming to birth they'll be the first to tell us about it. But out here on the frontier of the liberated areas, we Western types must learn to roll our own.

Our Vietnamese opponents possess a reputation for being suspicious. They certainly have the duty of suspecting political agreements brought by Westerners for their signature. But in fact no nation known to me is further from applying any principle of guilt by association. I can't think what people at war before has opened its heart to citizens of the aggressor power—and not merely revolutionaries boring from within, but uninfluential academic pacifists. So it happened that, during an involuntary period of leisure, like many others I had the shattering experience of receiving hospitality at the hands of the enemy, which has colored everything I've written here. If being given free access to Hanoi was propaganda, I wish

the United States would start propagandizing, on a scale proportionate to *her* resources, among her Socialist sisters.

When I began writing a year ago, I still found it necessary to
persuade myself that something had gone wrong, to trace each
tendril on the grapevine of dissent. Since then photographs of burning Washington, of counter-insurgency in Chicago have gone
around the world. I send the typescript to the press, knowing that
before it appears in print an American president will have been
inaugurated over the protest of American youth; but also that whatever action he takes on this unbelievable war, its damage to
America *will already have been done.* We will know and the world
will not forget that ours was a society whose institutions could offer
no effective resistance to genocide until it had been going on for
years.

We must fix it firmly in our minds that *saving face will not be
a change of heart.* The war wasn't an accident or a temporary
aberration. The counter-insurgency policy was fixed; the napalm,
CBU's, Huey Hogs, black boxes, etc., were stockpiled or lined up
in a development schedule; men stood ready to be slotted in at their
controls. It might have happened anywhere. In fact it is happening
and will continue to happen in many places. Viet Nam was the first
place somebody stood up and said No to us. Our first order of
business is digging down to the frame of mind in ourselves that
acquiesced in the ghetto and foreign adventures. I attempt here to
draw up a rough sketch map of the terrain.

(b) The fixed ground of our alienation

If radiation were killing our kids before our eyes or our enemy
were offering only nonviolent resistance, we'd have no doubt we
were on the wrong course. But it would be too late to change. If
we hope to act constructively, we can't ask for a clearer situation
than the one we're in. When I was little I had the idea that newspa-
per stories were about a different kind of people from us—unlucky
or important ones. But to pretend that we live in a neutral zone
where we can watch other people raise moral questions is finking
out. It won't do any longer to be recruited into prefabricated slots
—the only kind the alumni secretary knows how to record.

Every road, if you follow it to the end, leads into the middle of the city. Mysteriously, most of us don't follow any road; we need to be waked up into manhood. The situation is more critical than we realize until we investigate: the police are more brutal, the pollution of the Great Lakes has gone further. At the same time, things are more hopeful than we dared believe; without the newspapers having taken cognizance of it, a fluid liberated zone has been demarcated in the heart of occupied territory. For better or worse, things are more highly colored than we imagined them in our fallout shelter against history. All we have to do is go out and look. Nobody can do it for us.

Students have always put down the authorities, one way or another, in their persuasion that limitless possibilities lie ahead. Senior citizens, now as formerly, follow the road map to Retirement Mesa, and watch the shape of their death rise up like the Rockies across the plains. It's the middle-aged who're most conscious of living in revolutionary times, that the rules are being changed while they're playing. Such times used to be occasional, as in the sixteenth century, when a long overdue parcel of changes cracked the brittle institutions, and Catholic grandparents were stranded and useless bringing up Protestant grandchildren. But now we're stuck in the final phase of terrestrial evolution where a man dies in a very different climate from the one he was born in. By a Newton's Law of scientific discovery, the uniform force of curiosity produces a constant acceleration in the level of knowledge. I remember as a four-year-old looking at the front page of Lindbergh's Atlantic crossing spread out on the floor. Now my kids anticipate watching the first moon explorers on live space TV.

Summer cottages on Martha's Vineyard used to have out front a spherical mirror called a gazebo in which you could see nearly the whole universe. Recently they've all gotten smashed; we need a new model. This book is for people who've seen clearly that they're getting an unreliable picture—so clearly that no plausible TV commentator will ever be able to wrap them up again.

If you go back to the town where you were brought up and can't find it anymore, or don't fit in there now, you're alienated, a foreigner in the one place you thought you belonged. Not merely has it changed, so have you, and it's not easy to find a more suitable place. This uncertainty is the Gibraltar we build on.

If having gotten lost is alienation, a name for getting straightened out would be *naturalization:* the process (if any) by which we could work ourselves back into someplace we belong, an appropriate environment. The metaphor here comes in the first place from international law, where naturalization is a transfer of citizenship. We're driven to metaphor because we're not certain of the correct route; if we knew the route we'd already be taking it. The things that concern us most intimately can be defined only in the sense that the cowboy defines the steer by tossing a lasso at it.

The country you were born in is the most obvious label to describe where you belong. We grew up possessing citizenship in something called the United States of America. But in many ways it's become just a scene of exploitation, and the law it's so proud of only marks it as the inheritor of earlier imperialism.

By naturalization I mean, further, the process of regaining conditions of life clearly indicated by global biology; for exploitation is also directed against our past and against our natural environment. So far as we fail to find a citizenship, a historic continuity, a home on the planet, it's our right and duty to organize committees and send in our representatives to the Administration, however unsympathetic—demanding the right to take out first papers in an authentic society, to rediscover our tradition, to renew the ecological order.

Our awareness of alienation isn't generalized; it comes from quite particular things: sewage in streams, TV commercials, getting fired, black angry faces,

. . . guns and sharp swords in the hands of young children.

It's always connected with some kind of violence, with going against the grain of something. Most things are like wood; their parts are laid down in a definite direction; they have grain. It's violence to force people into jobs they don't want and won't be happy in. Violence is marked by inexpertness and impatience, as when children use screwdrivers for levers and bend them. Somebody is responsible for the alienation; it may be us. America hasn't got a monopoly on violence; but it's centered here, more dangerous, more accessible—and our responsibility.

B

The rest of this chapter analyzes the fixed starting point: our awareness of violence. Our inventiveness has escalated violence against the biological environment through pollution, overuse, industry; so far, the conservation movement hasn't achieved priority in our imaginations. The danger is at its most intense in the forms of proliferation: population explosion and nuclear explosion. In America also is centered a violence against oppressed populations; we've become the inheritors of colonialism at home and abroad. The counter-violence of liberation movements generated in our time at least has justice on its side. The technology which makes these kinds of violence possible becomes in its automation and mass-culture itself a violence against our tradition. The scene of this violence is an interlocking set of institutions which I call the Establishment. Our cue is to start counter-institutions operating inside it, where we can get our personal futures back in our own hands. The great sign of hope is the jelling of individuals into a Resistance. Violence came into being in the ancient world through freedom— and violence in turn elicited a new emergent out of freedom. The toxin generates its antitoxin.

In the succeeding chapters I've tried to compact stepping-stones, one at a time, in the four-dimensional chaos out of which is hatching the First World Revolution. Chapter II attempts to make ancient history, and in particular the Gospels, again available to us. Our rediscovery of imperialism makes the Roman Empire living history and renders the work of Jesus intelligible as a response to that exploitative society. Chapter III vindicates his revolutionary nonviolence as the appropriate response to our situation. His symbolism of the end of the world is seen as pointing in a genuine way to the meaning of technology. Chapter IV endeavors to put language about God at our disposal again as the natural way to describe the emergence of radical novelty in history.

Chapter V faces up to the fact that the tradition of the radical Jesus comes down to us in an Establishment Church. The contemporary Movement for peace and liberation is seen as the authentic bearer of the Spirit for our times, standing in a complementary relation to the Church. Church renewal and solidarity with the Movement are the key to each other. We see the beginnings of a *liberated Church in America,* carrying out resistance against the Establishment (including the official Church), above all in the area of conscription. For the purposes of our realistic action, that Liberated Zone is the most hopeful nucleus of Church reunion, social renewal, and environmental restoration, both here and on a planetary scale.

Of course it's presumptuous to think about these subjects. Even more presumptuous, for us inheritors of violence is not to think about them.

2. Violence against the biological environment

(a) Air and water pollution

When the air makes our eyes hurt or gives us asthma, we feel out of place. Something has gone wrong to produce the famous stink of Secaucus, N.J.—or the red vapor swirling around the floodlit shrubbery of Pasadena homes, like nitrous oxide in a retort. Ancient people thought the atmosphere was alive; certainly in our lungs it makes the difference between a live man and a dead one.

The atmosphere might be called the lungs of the biosphere— the mantle of life enveloping this planet. The proportions of oxygen and carbon dioxide regulate the balance between animals and plants, oxygen consumers and oxygen producers. Organic life and the air are interdependent results of planetary evolution.

Combustion of fossil fuels has perhaps increased carbon dioxide in the air 10 percent in this century. By a "greenhouse effect" this may warm the air enough to melt the polar icecaps one day and raise the sea level several hundred feet. Near our cancerously growing cities combustion adds other foreign products. The London fog, condensing around carbon particles from fireplaces, in bad weeks causes more deaths of heart and lung patients than acute poisonous fogs like the one of Donora, Pennsylvania, in 1948. The Los Angeles smog is a California novelty—a complex gas photosynthesized along the sunny freeways into greater toxicity, and mixed with the colloidal particles spun off from braking tires.

European history persuades us the city was meant to be the environment of "civilized" man. Our discomfort in Southern California proves we don't belong in these cities anyway; we're alienated from our environment. Medicine can only treat the symptoms. Air-conditioning purifies small volumes at the cost of burning fuel somewhere else to make electricity, and so polluting the air further. The problem isn't bad air but too many people. The atmosphere happened to be the commodity in shortest supply which gave out first—land could be cannibalized from orange groves, and water from the entire Southwest. (In Bombay, food gives out first; in Manhattan, space.) The foreseen heavier smog promises to increase the danger in unforeseeable ways; we know (even if we can't compute it) that a big enough concentration would make life impossible.

This is a spectacular local problem. But we can easily imagine ways to pollute the atmosphere overall—at once or through centuries—where the pollution could no longer be reversed by drying up the source. In a few years the atmosphere did throw off Krakatoa's explosion. This doesn't mean that, in the millions of years we should look forward to, it can keep absorbing a stream of the same pollutant.

Likewise there is little clean water left in America; industrial and animal wastes of all sorts are constantly being dumped into rivers, lakes, bays. If the atmosphere is our respiration, we can think of our waters as the circulatory system in an organism of fixed magnitude, a living spaceship. Two billion years of evolution have elaborately adjusted the habitat and its living occupants to each other. The compositions of seawater and soil are interrelated, the bee and the orchid that imitate it, forests and rainfall. We give the name *ecology* to the science which studies plants, animals, and the environment as an organic whole. Our economists haven't yet learned from the ecologists that a constantly expanding economy is unsuitable for a sphere of finite area.

(b) The environmental crises

The rapid spread of our species and its technology around the planet has produced in our century a whole series of *environmental crises*. Our treatment of air and water is only one feature of a massive *physical interference* with the environment; reversible, if caught in time. Thermal pollution near cities and factories destroys much of the original aquatic life. Perhaps two percent of continental United States has been waterproofed; the effects on water runoff and heating of the earth are as yet uncertain. Noise is also an environmental pollutant; the proposed supersonic transport will create regular sonic booms along its path, destroying our quiet, and with unknown long-term effects on other creatures.

A second type of environmental damage is *exploitation:* use of natural resources faster than they can be regenerated. Critical here is our use of phosphate fertilizers to maintain high population levels. Large-scale agriculture, sewage disposal, biodegradable detergents, all release phosphorus to streams and eventually to the sea-bottom, where it can be recovered only by dredging—or by waiting for the seabeds to rise. We continue to cut forests (including irreplaceable virgin stands) faster than they regrow. And it takes longer to restore soil than forest.

Most serious of all are *long-lived solid pollutants.* The sea bobs with indestructible objects—plastic bags, light bulbs, detergent bottles, rubber sandals, cork floats, ship timbers, orange crates—which the sorting action of currents concentrates on particular beaches. We must imagine the entire environment likewise filled with stable alien molecules. Oil slicks spread over coastal waters from wrecks like the *Torrey Canyon*, poisoning the water with phenolic compounds, keeping oxygen out of it, bogging down birds' feathers. DDT and other pesticides are extremely stable, their long-range effects are unknown; air and water currents, complex food chains have scattered them all over the earth—in the fat of Antarctic penguins, for example. Toxic lead salts show up in the Antarctic ice and everywhere else; they come apparently from anti-knock compounds in gasoline. Degradable only by time are radioactive fission products from nuclear explosions, with a wide spectrum of half-lives. All these items are being added to our habitat faster than they can be subtracted by natural processes.

(c) History of the environmental crisis

Why has environmental deterioration come to a head in Los Angeles? It's the frontier's end; beyond lie the crowded billions of China, Indonesia, India. Cultural innovations have spread east and west from their origin in the Levant, multiplying as they went, until after five millennia they met and recoiled in the Pacific theater of World War II. Technology hasn't any place to turn but in on itself.

Before the European's coming, the North American continent was so inaccessible that it lagged far behind Eurasia in its version of the Neolithic. The agricultural civilizations of Central America offered more resistance to colonizing than did the nomadic red men of the North, sparse like all predators. There wasn't any native culture here able to withstand the explosive bloom of technology.

Perhaps untidy man is descended from tree-dwelling primates, with a gravity system of garbage disposal and no need for the cat's instinctive cleanliness. Our Lady Macbeth compulsion is overcompensation—we keep washing our natural and artificial skins at the expense of filling the whole water table with detergent. Partly in an illusion of invisibility we think the environment will never notice us; partly with our lack of gentleness we will to impose our junk on the globe.

It's hard to learn that the solution to an old problem is a new one. Shall we fill the water table with desalinated seawater? We will build atomic power plants to supply the energy. Shall we seal the radioactive waste in concrete in the ocean? Let's not be surprised if some element turns out unexpectedly corrosive. Or rocket it off into space? There are the combustion products back in the air again. Shall we have big one-crop farms for efficiency? This encourages the crop's natural pest. We spray the fields with pesticide, which kills the birds that were helping us by eating them—and also breeds more resistant strains of the pest. A bigger dose will be needed next time.

A system of finite size can't put up with this escalation. In general the biosphere knows more than we do; many regulations are built into it we haven't learned. We know we can't rebuild the human body on a new basis; but the ecological balance is even more complicated—among many other things it includes us. In evolution's earlier course, as animals overgrazed some critical commodity they put a ceiling on their population, and so maintained the balance. Man is the animal that for a time can observe each scarcity or local pollution and patch it up; but only at the cost of introducing a bigger dislocation somewhere else. Our intelligence can merely delay judgment. We laugh at the primitive mind of the prophet who knows nothing more destructive than the sword; but his theorem is still valid, "All those who take the sword shall perish by the sword" (Matt. 26:52).

The impartiality of Nemesis induces us to give our bodies the same treatment as the rest of our environment. After everybody else had known it for a long time, finally the medical profession gathered statistics and announced what cigarettes were doing to our aerating apparatus. The thalidomide fiasco won't be forgotten for the seventy years its little victims (growing bigger) go around with prosthetic appliances, freely donated. Our self-congratulation grows thinner as we mobilize plastic surgeons to deal with the human detritus which was once southeast Asia's brown-eyed babies. Our chemicals are both a symptom and an attempted cure for the malaise of our alienation—gin, cigarettes, pot, aspirin, tranquilizers, LSD, barbiturates.

(d) The dynamic character of the disturbed balance

The stability envisaged by the ecologist is a doubly dynamic balance. To physical disturbances external or internal—a glacial or tropic age, a volcanic eruption—the system responds with damped rather than unstable oscillations. Imposed on this periodicity is the one-way track of evolution.

Human presence in the north temperate zone had set up a precarious new ecological balance. The Great Plains may have been created from forests by the wandering hunter, already a fire-animal. The farms of America and Europe have driven predators toward the less cultivable arctics and tropics. I have collected elsewhere historic records for the replacement of vast pine and oak forests in the Mediterranean by the grain, olive, fig, vine—and wasteland. Although we're far from knowing the long-term effect of these changes, they can provisionally be called legitimate adaptations to man, especially where Black Forests still stretch their fingers into hopfields and vineyards. But the Lebanon's mythopoeic eroded slopes today are no substitute for the great forest of cedar and Cilician fir which survived at least one pluvial period. And the gross dislocations mentioned previously make every kind of adjustment difficult or impossible.

Still man wasn't meant to fit invisibly into a hypothetical climax vegetation sheltering all its original fauna; the logic of his development was bound to make a big difference. It's remarkable that old records should see this so clearly: "Be fruitful and multiply, fill the earth and subdue it, have dominion over the animals" (Gen. 1:28). The myth of the garden which the species Adam was to till and keep looks to the future, not the past. Eden is the name of the earth as it should become in view of the radical novelty we represent. In arid deforested Greece, the mythology of nymphs and dryads isn't the country as it was, but as it was meant to be.

(e) Man's role in guiding planetary development

The successive phases of evolution and history, while they degrade solar energy, keep producing greater complexities of organization, of psychic energy. Viewing time's one-way arrow, our language inevitably speaks of the process by analogy with human will. Human purposiveness is a fairly advanced illustration of a general principle, because it's one result of the process. But it is not the most advanced, for evolution won't stop tomorrow. No human will conceived the idea of human society, or set in motion the exponential accumulation of science.

Man shouldn't have to coexist with the saber-toothed tiger, the malarial mosquito, the tapeworm. But big predators are more easily exterminated. It was too bad that the wild ox (the "unicorn" of the King James Bible) and the Siberian mammoth had to go. If the lion or the polar bear, the kangaroo or the hippo, should also fall by the way, something of us will die; they stand for complexes of energy built into the childhood of the race or our childhood. Just as the individual's embryonic development recapitulates the whole development of life, society maintains living vestiges of all its earlier phases. Whatever new is developed, we can't dispense with something like the parish, the guild, the city-state, the neolithic farmstead. On the deepest level, each of us has a solitary Paleolithic man inside him that needs the wilderness to hunt and fish or take pictures in. Besides providing that psychic space for us, the wilderness is a balance wheel to iron out our mistakes. And we also have a duty to the moose and carnivores, which need a lot of room and have their own claim to existence.

Although in the long run these are the most critical problems that face us, they never have to be solved by tomorrow morning; and so something else always takes priority. The authorities concerned put the problems in manila folders, and hire scientists and lobbyists to slap restrictions on somebody else. We outsiders know that a lot of things should be done right away, until our natural reactions have been masked by chamber-of-commerce camouflage. If we shall ever learn to use care and feeling where we cultivate intensively, to leave wilderness areas alone, we must acquire *a piety toward the natural order:* a whole new content to our religion or philosophy or whatever the thing is that we have.

3. Violence by proliferation

(a) The population explosion as ethnic competition

Every symptom in our degradation of nature has one root: too many people. As our planning breaks through the upper limit on the population of every non-intelligent species, we dominate the environment by our technological presence. Potentially the biggest threat is radioactive fission products of medium half-life—fallout from aerial explosions or waste from reactors. By analogy with biological proliferation, we can speak of proliferation of atomic weapons from big countries to medium ones to little ones, with growing danger of slip-ups. We may sum up as *global proliferation* the massive threat to the environment presented by explosions of physical atoms and of the atoms of society.

The Hindu father with a numerous starving progeny has no vision of a balanced earth. We who do, still imagine the dominant strain in that harmonious mankind as persons physically like ourselves. This genetic competition won't ever produce a stabilized planetary population. Australians and Americans have assumed a white man's burden to increase and multiply over a continent at the expense of the aborigines. French Canucks speak of *la vengeance de la crèche*, defeating with the cradle those who defeated them with the sword. The Palestinian refugees multiply faster than the U.N. can resettle them, and trust the world's conscience to feed them, in the blind faith that one day they'll be numerous enough

to spill back over their own frontiers. Harlem and Puerto Rican
Manhattan keep spreading through simple acceptance of a minimal
standard of living.

Genetic aggression is the remaining counter-imperialist
weapon of the oppressed world. American demographers are currently recommending the Loop or other inter-uterine devices to
Asiatic and Latin American governments. Black nationalists see
this as another form of genocide: "You give white women a pill to
have quadruplets, and black women a pill to make them sterile."
In fact, the governments implanting the Loop want to raise the
standard of living and start industrializing like us. And we can deal
better with industrial competition than with peasant fertility. So
population planning, though critically necessary, has been corrupted into another tool of neo-colonialism. It's not so much a
horde of people as a yellow horde we're afraid of. The remedy
which we provide at home by individual appointment to families
is prescribed overseas by shotgun to entire provinces. We must
reform our imaginations and stop the war before we can ask its
victims to give up their ultimate weapon—even though it's as dangerous in the long run as ours.

The strength of a species lies in its plasticity, in the range of
latent variations in its genetic pool. It's too late for the giraffe to
take on a new habitat. We presume that in man also mixture of
genetic strains gives strength; we know the converse is true—in-
breeding in small communities brings out recessive defects like
Appalachian feeble-mindedness and the hemophilia of European
royalty. We're surer of the social analogy, that the most interesting
societies—ancient Greece, Elizabethan England—have been the
product of many cultures. We should always have available traditional hardy communities of farmers or fishermen to introduce
fresh cultural strength into an effete society, and probably actual
genetic strength. In any case we can count on the miscegenated
toughs educated in the school of the street, the fittest survivors of
the ghetto jungle.

(b) Proliferation of nuclear explosions

Beside the few million dollars allocated to population control is a better-funded answer to human proliferation, the proliferation of atomic bombs outward from Los Alamos. A sheet called "California Living" shows a gang of typical American kids sitting on some defused nuclear devices in the patio of the Los Alamos museum. The exhibits have an attractive bulging pod-shape and are painted white. I don't know how many of our California Japanese families have made a vacation pilgrimage there. (The patriotic acquiescence of the Japanese to temporary detention in 1941 is a source of quiet local pride: "Isn't it too bad we had to do to them what we did; but didn't they take it well?") No other nation would use quite this chummy prose on the subject:

> In the weapons display is "Fat Man," a chunky bomb with a menacing snout. It is the favorite of young bomb climbers.
> When "Little Boy" was dropped on Hiroshima on Aug. 6, 1945, it took a toll of 78,150 dead; 37,425 injured; 13,983 missing. It is one of the smallest bombs and has a core no bigger than a portable typewriter.

In the face of our willingness to take the unknown risks of underground nuclear blasts for releasing natural gas, of atomic power plants blowing up (which nearly happened near Detroit in October, 1966), of atomic ships sinking, of our deterrent force actually being used, the ribbon loops up in this portable typewriter and jams on the reels. We retain freedom of speech to state in America that the frame of mind which accepts these paragraphs leads to genocide. One would have gotten into trouble for saying so in Nazi Germany—which just goes to show that our Establishment has neutralized freedom better than theirs. That little fellow with the Marine haircut sitting on Fat Man has strontium 90 in his baby teeth. I happen to know, because the mummy of some kids like him takes the teeth that the spiders take from under the pillows and sends them off to a laboratory. Will somebody please explain to me what all our mummys and daddys can be thinking about?

(c) Proliferation as self-defeating

The increase of our species overloads the ecological pyramid and weakens the whole structure underneath us. Nuclear war may render the biological habitat uninhabitable, or reduce it to a distorted and degenerate level. However unreasoning and blind the population explosion, it's at least a form of life. More blast and radiation is an American kind of answer to more human bodies. We're forced to meet the Orient on their ground, fighting with a disproportionately black army—conscripted native troops. The Chinese nuclear tests show they plan to meet us on *our* ground.

The twin forms of proliferation are monstrous offspring of the pride which ancient books, Eastern and Western, see as the wellspring of our troubles. Each is the arrogant claim to impose our will on the planet. The central message of past wisdom is the inevitable destruction of such arrogance by an agency variously described as God, the Gods, the nature of things, human nature. Today for the first time the sequences of cause and effect by which judgment will be executed in history's tribunal are plain to everybody. The tradition is ambiguous how far those relatively guiltless will escape; for all we know the planet will be the innocent bystander that gets it in the neck.

Natural processes had to reduce background radiation very low before we could come along. In a state of nature, any child can see how many muskrat belong in each brook, how many deer can feed in a field. Statistics is our most American science. We have too much of everything to count; we ourselves at somewhere over 200 million are way overcrowded already. Our works should be as organic to the landscape as the beaver-dam. Our real problem isn't mismanagement of our surroundings but of ourselves. The historic task of our age is to throw away Frodo's ring of power.

Conservationists have said that people are more important than trees; but judging from ease of replacement we may say, *trees are more important than people.* On our planetary space-voyage without destination we've got to be good stewards of the built-in resources for the absentee dispatcher. In our alleged "mastery over nature," we, who can't make one hair black, have used up irrecoverably certain minerals, lakes, species to build our current unsatisfactory society. Our cue is to slow down and rethink goals. Legislation is necessary, but it'll be both tyrannical and ineffective unless it represents personal convictions. On a free planet, population planning must spring from family planning; long-term conservation must rely on kids who love birds and frogs. Conformity to our nature can only be defined by a word that hasn't been spoken in the West for hundreds of years now: moderation.

4. Violence in the human family: the oppressed

(a) The United States as inheritor of colonialism

No upheaval in the subhuman order—the extinction of the dinosaurs, earthquake or glaciation, the chain of animals preying on each other—prepares us for the San Andreas fault running across human society. Any myth or ideology must come to terms with the fact that most, but not quite all, human beings fall far short of humanity. (How we can say so is a further puzzle.) The level of technology that's made damage to nature grossly visible in our generation has equally magnified mutual antagonisms. We live in a very special time when all the world's chickens are coming home to roost. The geography of escalating violence to man closely parallels violence to nature. Both follow the diffusionist pattern of technology, spreading from a single point of discovery.

North America, the least advanced continent in 1600, is most advanced today. East of the Levant, early trade routes produced Mesopotamian-style cultures in the river valleys of the Indus, the Yangtze, the Hwang. Tenacious backward imperial civilizations developed, resistant to technology precisely because of their monsoon-soaked fertile plains, mild winters, endlessly repeating villages. The introduction of Western medicine by humanitarian missionaries, especially in India, aggravated or began the Malthusian cycle of famine and overpopulation. Enormous economic and political forces then worked to prevent the industrialization of lands once colonized. The British Raj in India, whatever its merits, principally bore in upon the ruled their incapacity for self-government. As political colonialism was replaced by a more powerful economic colonialism—the fly-whisk giving way to the Coke bottle —the role of the oppressed was unchanged. Carl Oglesby's data and rhetoric in his chapters of *Containment and Change* present an

overwhelming case that what we call the Free World is the area
of American business enterprise, which relegates the colonial world
to exporting raw materials and importing manufactured items. Our
industrialism presupposes that we've inherited the role of colonial
power; hence it's unavailable for the poor nations that we theoretically offer it to.

"The poor you have always with you" (Mark 14:7), but both
relatively and absolutely they are worse off than ever before—and
sorted out in space by the ever-widening gap between the industrial
and non-industrial countries. We may take affluent California and
the impoverished Orient as emblematic, facing each other across
the misnamed Pacific. Not merely are the countries of the Far East
poor, they've been dislocated and corrupted by us. At the same
time we've necessarily corrupted ourselves, in a deeper way. If any
ideology or religion wants us to take its claim of moral concern
seriously, it will begin by condemning the injustice done by the rich
to the poor.

(b) Viet Nam as focus of colonialism

The name of injustice—the violence exercised by the strong
on the weak—today is colonialism. In any future we can imagine,
a necessary (if not sufficient) condition of justice will be anti-colonialism. Africa and South America have as yet no big brothers to back
them up, so the first action was joined across the Pacific. Japan
wasn't really an Oriental country; she made the mistake of being
an industrial nation, challenging us on our own ground, opening
a way for us to declare war on her; and so world opinion let us
overwhelm her with the cornucopia of our power. But the true
representative of the Orient couldn't make these mistakes. We
failed to note the wisdom of the British in withdrawing from Asia,
the defeat of the French at Dien Bien Phu, their extrication from
Algeria. We let ourselves be trapped into defending our prestige
or our investments where we couldn't declare war; where we had
to appear as the aggressor, grant the enemy a sanctuary from land
invasion, keep up a paper-thin pretense of avoiding civilian targets.

And so it has happened that Viet Nam, the home of a culture
underground for two millennia and now physically driven under-

ground, a place Americans had barely heard of and had certainly not expected to visit as enemy or friends, has become the center of world history in our time: the place where the tide of colonialism is turning. It might have seemed the most vulnerable part of Southeast Asia to the West—the only nation with a Roman script, deeply Catholicized, with a strong impress of French colonial administration. More recently it has taken on Marxism; but it has adapted each of those things to its native spirit. The heroine of the national epic "Kieu," constantly getting put to service in the green pavilion to rescue her father from debtors' prison, ends her days in a platonic relationship with her original lover. Her autumnal fidelity has been transformed into a single-minded resistance, sparing neither itself nor its enemy, which can be recognized as the vanguard of the revolutionary world.

Viet Nam and America can never ignore each other again, the rings of our destinies are interlocked. You have a special knowledge of the first kid that stood up to your bullying and licked you. Our enemy is one of the remoter societies from us in diet, physique, culture, and way of thinking; our minds are rapidly being expanded. The reality of that encounter is a glass we can see ourselves in:

> Mirror mirror on the wall
> Who is hated most of all?

It would be unfair if only the imaginative or the drafted could receive that knowledge by meeting the other side face to face. But the universe is not unfair; nobody is condemned without a chance to cross-examine his accusers. From the day we landed here, the truths about ourselves we're being taught in Asia have been available at home.

(c) The ghetto as colonial enclave

Look at the map of the American city, so familiar and instructive. As its center gets dilapidated, the office-managers move out to the suburbs, taking first their churches with them, then their offices. Rent and tax policies prevent the fall of land values which would let the city buy its heart back for parks or civic centers. It becomes profitable for landlords to subdivide and rent to immi-grants from Europe or Asia, Latin America, and above all from the black rural South. This invading guerrilla band drives out remaining middle-class amenities; it's controlled by a few strategic points in the hands of the colonialists—city hall, precinct stations, courts, clinics, welfare. To link the command posts in the occupied subur-ban territory, a circular freeway is drawn around the center, with emplacements of supermarkets, gas stations, discount houses, bowl-ing alleys, redemption centers, liquor stores, drive-ins. Outside is a no-man's-land, a green belt, and then the landscaped martini-strewn hills. This circle is a hangman's noose constricting an ever larger population into the central ghetto. If the city began as a seaport like Newark or Oakland, part of the noose is replaced by the shoreline, fenced off and polluted by freeways or rotting docks.

On either side of the frontier we're made to feel out of place. Up on the hill, the sprinkled lawns and power-clipped hedges fence off each two-car family, which boycotts its neighbors and drives off a safe distance for school, office, club, nightclub. Down on the flatlands we find the community we missed higher up, but in an atmosphere of resignation, bitterness, or grim social climbing. The hill people keep the tuition high in the private colleges, and the standard exacting in the better state universities; they appropriate funds away from the ghetto schools. Only their own kids can pass the symbolic hurdle of education that gives the degree that awards the advertising job that cheats the public that pays the salary that maintains the house on the hill. The City Zoning Commission chart is the field map of a relentless class warfare.

In the idealistic days of the Civil Rights Movement we had the impression we were building an integrated society. Driving past the charred storefronts of Springfield Avenue in Newark one sees that, whatever we accomplished, it wasn't that. With talent, hard work, luck, and willingness to fink out, the elite of a colonialized people can pass over to their oppressors. But that doesn't change where the bulk of their community is at. There must be a black community before it can shake hands with the white community.

Our conviction about the basic decency of our motives is a kind of front lawn kept for show: every day we look out the window

and see more crabgrass and say, "Someday we must root it all out."
But one morning we'll look out and discover there isn't any lawn
there anymore, no background of basic decency, just crabgrass.

In this century there was still a little band of free Indians in
Oregon, sustained by their knowledge that their land was their own
and their cause just. With the last of them, Ishi, whose true name
was never learned, there died some piece of wisdom about living
on this continent. Buffy Sainte Marie has written their National
Anthem after the fact:

My country 'tis of thy people we're dying.

When we brought the African here to work in the red man's place,
we gave him a better title to the land than we held ourselves.

We're trying to boost the black man up to our level so we can
stucco and paint over the crack in the Great Society and present
a solid front to the world. The Greeks in a mythical genealogy said
that folly begat repletion, repletion begat arrogance, and arrogance
begat Nemesis—getting what you deserve. In the wisdom of their
pre-scientific world view they didn't localize justice outside or inside us, they just said it was there. Freud sees an accurate mech-
anism finding a symbolic outlet for the hatred whose direct
expression is blocked. Nobody likes to meet Truth or Judgment,
which shuffle onto history's minstrel show in blackface.

This nation was founded by religious refugees who'd learned
only too much from their persecutors. What led the seventeenth-
century Puritans into moral error, unable to read their Bibles
beyond the book of Joshua? Englishmen were conscious of surfing
on the wave of a cultural dynamism: they were producing a supreme world-literature; they'd passed through the cataclysm of the
Reformation (even so not thorough enough); in Newton for the first
time they were describing the actual workings of the universe;
dimly ahead they could see rising up the Industrial Revolution, the
British Empire. And so they closed the book, unwilling to read any
further and find out that the only way to fulfill their destiny was
to become servants of the wretched of the earth.

The reward of having climbed higher in the evolutionary scale
or the historic process is that ever more difficult decisions are

c

presented to us, with corresponding punishments for failure. "You only have I known of all the families of the earth; therefore I will visit upon you all your iniquities." The Fall of Man today is localized in colonialism. The Eskimo and the Tahitian hadn't really come out from Eden when we first saw them. Did they really need the Gospel? They did after having been visited by the planter, the rumrunner, the colonial administrator. We'd like to believe in an even higher virtue than their innocence, with the power of self-defense; we know *we* haven't got it.

(d) The scope of the exploitation

The black here welcomes anything useful white men can do with their own people; but he knows that any gift we make to him we've also got the power to recall. Freedom that's granted isn't freedom, because it can also be rescinded. The only real freedom is the kind that's been won, made a personal possession.

Our initial move toward reality is listening to what black faces are saying. I saw clearly from the Middle East, when the late Malcolm X had his big success there, that the tide of African nationalism was rising and falling—mostly rising—in rhythm with the freedom movement here. There was some kind of hot line between Selma and Khartoum. Every time a sheriff got out the tear gas, dogs, and cattle-prods, pictures went on front pages all around the world.

When the Afro-American first met with people from the National Liberation Front of South Viet Nam—it was at Bratislava—what he said to them was this:

> We the black people have only suffered under one imperialist power, unlike you; but we also are colonialized. It is not our job to give our brothers in arms advice, but to help; to disrupt American society by any means necessary. We support the liberation struggle wholeheartedly. The United States has been unapproachable and unteachable; our choice is to destroy it or face genocide.

We've got a revolution on our hands. Watts, Hunter's Point, Jersey

City, are a little bit of overseas, an enclave of colonialism where we can be imperialists at home. They resist being co-opted because they have a message for their brothers; they've got to retain integrity not only for themselves but for three other continents as well. The British, French, Dutch, could divest themselves of their imperial possessions; we brought ours home and we're stuck with them.

The infection has come to fever crisis in our own times for the same reason as the ravaging of the planet; the circle of the nations has been closed up; we see facing us across the Pacific the accusing victims we thought we'd left behind across the Atlantic. To keep the expansion booming that Fortress America relies on, we must export our products to the poor world, but not our technology. And we haven't merely accepted our historical role, we've accepted it gladly. Carl Oglesby shows how deeply we've gotten into the economics and politics of countries like Brazil. The suggestion hasn't been made that they should play the same role in our affairs.

Our treatment of the red man, the black man, the yellow man, the poor man, has been gratuitously contemptuous; for anybody that believes Freud or fears God it bears the unmistakable pockmarks of guilt. For what crime or sin? Not simply wealth; not simply that we're on the growing edge of scientific development— although both helped push us over the cliff. History and geography put us in the position where it was easy to exploit nature, first on this continent, then globally; easy to exploit what the Germans call the nature-peoples. After we tried exploitation and observed its advantages, we decided we liked it; we chose to continue it. Guilt lies in having chosen to accept guilt.

The violence we're doing isn't against a harmony between classes or nations that's ever been fully realized in history. But the contrasts are sharper today than ever before. Our technological wealth (itself based on shortsighted exploitation of nature) spotlights the injustice of unequal distribution. We can't bring ourselves to look for a genuine way of beginning redress. And so we defend the injustice, attributing our affluence to the merits of our economic system, our religion, our character, our ancestry, our tradition.

Does a self-knowledge still coexist somewhere with all this

self-deception? Perhaps in our better mind we know that all men are in principle citizens of a single commonwealth. How did we get the United Nations into our pocket—edging it into Manhattan safe from lobbying by unauthorized liberation fronts, keeping the biggest country on earth out of it? The U.N. is nowhere near good enough for a permanent fatherland. But if we became willing to accept the burden of our guilt, in some metaphorical or actual sense we'd be transferring our loyalties to a universal citizenship. Our cue is to find a way of applying for naturalization—taking out papers in the commonwealth, whatever it may be, where our true citizenship lies.

5. Violence against our tradition

(a) The manipulative society

When I flew in from Beirut in the summer of '65 after seven years overseas, I went through a severe reentry shock. All at once I was supposed to deal with direct distance dialing, zipcodes, Marshall McLuhan, marinas, automobile seat belts, flowpens, the Jefferson Airplane, individual parent-teacher conferences, Dean Rusk, games people play, Captain Kangaroo, credit cards, the death of the Twentieth Century Limited, nuclear power plants, carrying my draft card, programmed learning, Walter Cronkite, pop art, electric toothbrushes, defensiveness, and ignorance. I failed—that instructive failure which everybody deserves to have once.

Most of all the man from Mars or Peace Corps returnee is stumped by the required expertise at conformity. He must expose himself to sensitivity training at a leadership skills institute, and next day admire the academic know-how of the people at defense think tanks. One month Hawaiian cocktails are all the thing; the next, it's traditional native Mexican delicacies. He's got to read consumer magazines: "There are all these wonderful things in the stores and you can't afford to pass them up, but you have to know what you're buying and where to get it." His kids are subjected to inkblots in school *and* vulgarized set theory *and* open interpersonal relations, while all the time he knows his kids' friends' folks voted against open housing.

As our small-town childhood, the comforting apolitical subjects we studied, have gone the way of the trolley car, the Bay ferry, the Boston local, and the Grange social, the vacuum is filled by what we may classify as advertising. The conspicuous features of our public life were devised to be reported: news conferences, prizefights, Congressional hearings, political conventions, policy speeches. Airstrikes over underdeveloped countries are conducted for the benefit of plucky TV cameramen; they're envisaged as spectaculars to dramatize our retaliatory capacity. (But then the policeman must be invited to school—where *we* never saw him—and lay down ground rules when to copy the violence of the silver screen and when not.)

Manipulation is king. Our universities are begetting associated research institutes that simulate counter-insurgency and recovery from nuclear attack. The automation and flow control of our factories, banks, post offices, airports are making us superfluous appendages to our master Social Security punch card somewhere. University graduates are channeled into the bags where somebody wants them by the carrot of projected salary curve, the club of induction, the trap of psychological testing. Our clergy are assured in their pastoral charges that the spirit of prophecy lies in enabling their congregations to do what they'd wanted to do all along. The shape of what is called contemporary literature is determined by the need of highspeed presses for a regular sequence of best sellers.

We all need to have some leverage on the future through the monuments of our own past. But the word has gone out that Elizabethan English is irrelevant for our generation. This brought an eight-year-old I know to tears, who adores the tongue in which Robin Hood and hobbits converse. She's sitting there in church with her thumb in the Epistle when a different book gets opened up. It doesn't sound like Epistles and the minister keeps stumbling. "It is not the function of the Church to teach children the language of Shakespeare." Nor anybody else's function; and after Shakespeare, Milton in high school will enter the same oblivion as high school Latin, college Greek, and seminary Hebrew.

Language is the normal way of organizing our experience, and our frustration with *Time* and *Life* also attests violence against natural order. Their columns are written in an itchy fiddling with the mother tongue, not the spoken idiom of any class of society, but a gravelly conglomerate of nonce phrases from the mortician, the ad man, the film critic, the interior decorator, the TV interviewer. Although this patois may save space, and in addition be considered distinctive, it's mainly functional; an idiom is required in which the burning of a village can naturally be described as pacification.

In the unreality of our consumer society, the dishwasher and disposal only liberate the lady of the house for more hairdos and discussion groups. By its non-functionality it generates inner contradictions, today's adaptations are tomorrow's maladjustments. Patriotic rationing is replaced by knowing consumption. The businessman's inner punctuality is turned against his body in the time-change of jet travel. Our imagined tranquility when the last child marries is punctured by the recreation adviser at the Florida retirement community. The zenith of America is the wilderness casino of Lake Tahoe, erecting its neon signs against the frosty stars, parasitic on an ostentatious society, discharging its garbage into the crystal waters and breeding algae—an elaborate non-culture, non-community, non-environment.

There aren't any more neutral academic topics. Experts on southeast Asian linguistics, elementary particles, corporation sociology, urban crime, Protestant theology, suddenly have to decide whether they'll accept research grants from a tax-exempt foundation (laundering CIA dollars), or get shoved over the edge. *Nobody is being left alone.* Junior high school principals are begging the student body officers to sit on committees and prop up the system. Nothing is sacred to leisure or scholarship; all is up for grabs. A *cultural totalitarianism* has set in. But what this means is, the Judgment is at hand. Nothing is secular; every area is subject to moral claims.

It's the teen-agers who see through it, because they're the ones that have to enter it from outside. Brought up in those tough plastic bags up on the hill, with every lesson in playing the game of affluence, they're breaking through and becoming dropouts or activists. Neither the drug scene nor the street scene necessarily shows the way to a renewed society. But at least they're a finger pointing at the reality of violence here and overseas, a clumsy lunge beyond alienation. American society is being rejected by the most interesting of its youth. A cry has gone out for restoring contact with the past, the tradition embodied in the torch-race of the generations.

(b) The hope of naturalization

In my father and my son I see another me occupying a different segment on time's arrow. Our best clue to the mystery of time is the family drama, the history of Oedipus or Lear or Faulkner's dynasties. But without wealth or fanaticism I can't invent a self-perpetuating family tradition. There will always be tension between father and son, as between man and man, so long as we're competing for air to breathe and a place in the sun. But once it existed within a common culture; there were presuppositions about what families did with their work-hours and play-hours. The speedup in the rate of innovation, which as we saw has alienated man from nature and from his brother, has also alienated man from his father.

The poets and spiritual leaders whom we trust are learned men; they've gone to school with the masters of tradition, the old books of our race. But we can't afford to take the truth at second hand from them. If a plant has been uprooted nothing will do but to put it back in its earth again. We possess a proper biological environment; it isn't infinitely plastic, it changes only by its own laws, which we can partly understand. We have a proper social environment, and the polarization of rich and poor does violence to both. Beneath both biology and society is the stream of awareness by which we grasp what it means to be a biological and political animal: the tradition which constitutes our cultural environment.

6. The Establishment as the scene of violence

(a) Establishment as supra-personal will

We all have the will to violence. We also need the camouflage of seeming to do something else, which is provided by the alleged aims of the institution we operate in. Under the same umbrella we find the power to implement our private vindictiveness, which

would otherwise be impotent. The institution has its own momentum; at the end of a war we do things we'd have blushed for at the
beginning—the logic of our commitments requires it.

Did we sign up for the institution without reading the fine
print? Or did we figure correctly that we could use it as an extension
of our personality, lend ourselves to its purposes? It couldn't organize isolated wills into something bigger than any of them, and
provide a pretext for their violence, unless it were performing an
apparently necessary function. The claim to absolute legitimacy by
a hereditary monarch, a party, a Church, a research institute, a
permanently democratic government, authorizes it to commit bigger crimes than more casual institutions. Industry has the self-
evident legitimacy of making money, supported by the claim of
conforming to a correct economic system. An army has the evident
legitimacy of power—perhaps too evident, so that it adds the symbolic legitimacy of bunting, civil ritual, the claim to be a school of
democracy.

A Great Power presupposes cooperation among its institutions
—the bureaucratic apparatus, heavy industry, the armed forces, the
mass media, the Church or party, the universities, the financial
managers. No matter how revolutionary, it will raise up a ruling
class whose sons climb the parallel ladders; no matter how conservative, new blood will break into power. The ladders intersect.
Retired Air Force generals show up on the boards of aerospace
industries; talented administrators shuttle between the university,
tax-exempt foundations, and advisory levels of government.

This monolithic political-industrial-military-intellectual-prop-
agandist complex is what I call an Establishment. Its interlocking
sectors hold all effective power; they seem not so much to rule the
society as to *be* the society. *It* escalates violence; nobody else has
the resources. *Its* industry and wars pollute the environment; *its*
elite perpetuate colonialist policies; *its* media supplant a traditional
culture by something more useful; *its* extra-legal agencies claim the
bodies of our young men. No person or group forms its policy.
Some purposiveness both more and less than human has taken it
over; we may call it the *scene* of violence.

In different ways both the American liberal and revolutionary avoid the fact that exploitation is done through the institutions of their own society. The liberal, who won't see how far the damage has gone, pretends the general violence is a bundle of distinct problems, each of which will yield to reason. The revolutionary, who refuses to see how far he still benefits, pretends this isn't his society, that by some easily-defined change in administration the corruption will disappear. Violence also coexists with much apparent personal freedom—for the white middle class. Our Establishment is a new phenomenon in scale: it is so big and powerful that until recently it hasn't felt threatened by freedom, which just fills up the holes between one big violence and another, like sand in a bag of marbles.

Its subtlest strength is its claim to weakness: it needs our support to avoid anarchy. This is like the law of gravity pleading for our ratification. In any foreseeable future here we'll want less centralized government, not more. Few further results are to be expected from bringing Federal pressure to bear on Southern whites. If the Establishment is so inflexible that it has to mobilize all its resources behind every disastrous policy, that's its problem —we may not be able to assist.

(b) The Establishment generates a Resistance

We're kidding ourselves if we think we can look around and find a large-scale organization of society overwhelmingly better than ours. If we fly to a socialist country we won't escape conscription. In fact there will be fewer avenues for conscientious objection (but partly because fewer consciences need object to what their military is doing). Students in New York or Paris legitimately protest they can't make decisions affecting their own future; the brief 1968 springtime in Prague showed the same unrest. The United States and Russia have converged to a similar balance between state control and private enterprise. To reduce the violence-level would take, not a shift in methods of control, but a radical alteration in the kind of enterprise we are running.

It's difficult to believe or explain how we went so far wrong. Even if everybody in Washington or Moscow were infallible computers, the system is too big for them to control even on their own terms. And we're not a different species from our leaders. Any possible liberation of American society would have to include agrarian revival, decentralization. And this isn't going to be planned; it will happen if at all by forces out of our control.

Establishment liberals call the cry for peace and liberation anarchistic because they can't see the extent of the danger. Actual contact with the realities of violence around the globe—war, deforestation, fallout, the ghetto, starvation, revolt—has persuaded this observer that our Establishment is culpably wrong; it has taken pains to shut its eyes. The problem isn't in maintaining what is called law and order here, but in fending off world collapse. People ought to be resigning from high place in Government, Church, industry; they aren't. Of all people, it's often the retired generals who are both realistic and secure enough to see the truth.

The force of sanity in our society isn't some movement for conservation or return to traditional wisdom. In phases it's been positive—the civil rights movement to pass and enforce certain legislation, community organizing to build a base of the dispossessed on the foundation of self-interest. But on balance it's been negative, a loose-jointed and formidable *resistance*, sometimes nonviolent, sometimes destructive, always ignored at our peril; saying No in Berkeley to academic bureaucracy, No in Detroit to a hopeless future, No in the Haight-Ashbury to a hypocritical moralism, No at the Pentagon to extermination. We straight middle-class types would have predicted and preferred that the cry against exploitation take a different form; but since we were silent, our cue is to accept thankfully what Providence has provided. (If the Attorney General thinks there's a nation-wide conspiracy, I wish he'd give us its address so we could go and get orders from it.)

The massive sign of strength is a movement for peace and freedom, born in a thousand places and envisaging a whole spectrum of opponents—an apparently indissoluble combination of neurosis and Gandhiism. The great peace demonstrations of 1967 had a deliberately non-exclusionist policy; every group was invited to help formulate the call and come do its thing. Many of its leaders think it must stay oriented around particular issues, non-ideological, pluralistic. I believe that phase is coming to an end; as it finishes organizing its primary constituency, an institutional shape emerges willy-nilly, and our task is to build all the flexibility and safeguards into its institutions we can.

(c) Initial thoughts on resistance

Where can we act responsibly in this critical and unprecedented situation? The "responsible citizen" is said to support the State's current goals even while he looks for others it might conceivably adopt. But it's beyond the powers of the State we know to envisage, much less begin, an end to violence; the key goals of the State are precisely what we can't support. In the Third World of Latin America, Asia, parts of Africa, revolution to create a new State makes good sense or the only sense. In America, even the formation of an effective third party seems beyond our strength; if revolution happens it'll be the work of black militants who mayn't be responsive to outside suggestions about their aims or methods. To save the planet, the oppressed, our own souls, the first priority is to set up a solid wall of resistance against violence at each of the critical points; otherwise the damage will go on until automatic reaction sets in. If there's a positive reconstruction it'll happen in unsuspected ways as a result of our having held the line. We aren't clever or pure enough to look into the future; the job where we are is to man the dykes against the tides of Leviathan.

Responsible citizenship has come to a dead end. The exploitative society is setting aside token national parks, devising token medical relief for napalmed children. King's assassination solidified the Poor People's Campaign; the reader will be able to judge whether it has forced more than a token response. We go through symbolic motions of political participation in hope of a better day. The State has taken on the dream-role of the mad doctor with the poisoned hypodermic who catches up with us as our legs refuse to function. If we as individuals don't take responsibility for ultimate problems—not remote but desperately at hand—nobody will. Of course, since our individuality is a network of personal relations, that means operating inside the network. We will work most effectively within groups which embody maximum agreement among the convictions of their members. A conviction is something we've worked out inside an alert and sympathetic group, and tested in action.   /

We can't replace the State and its violence by a better-ordered society. We can't find some special air uncontaminated by its poisons, consumer goods uncorrupted by its planned obsolescence, a police force (local or global) free of its brutality. And if we tried we couldn't guarantee that our replacement would not in its turn become an Establishment. In the dilemma of revolutionary counter-violence, our cue is to operate in a different realm: to work through groups which refuse to be the State and symbolically represent a better order of things—resisting her encroachments, putting constant pressure on her, opening up avenues of change in the right direction. We have a better chance of building permanent principles of self-reform into such a counter-Establishment.

Wherever violence has gone so far as to corrupt the unescapable framework of nature and society, we suffer along with all the rest. But its root is a violence each man does to himself, and here our power is unalienable. Not symbolically but actually anybody can reverse violence in that realm by standing up and confessing himself a man, by saying with a Dave Harris, "Hell no—I won't go." Nonviolence on this level won't mend nature or society unless it spreads—but its characteristic is to spread, and anyway it is what it is.

7. Violence and freedom

(a) The self-negation of violence

Until recently, violence against society had not been accompanied by violence against nature. Hitler represents a transitional phase, not to be repeated, where the inhuman policies of the present were still worked out with the means of the past. On the political scene, his refinements of violence were directed against his own citizens (and neighbors he claimed for his own). He did no worse to England than she to him; and even Coventry and Dresden only set the stage for our appearance. With us in charge, the miniaturized Viet Nam police action was assumed without question to call for defoliants, and the trees are dying around Saigon airport just from leakage. On America's tombstone we shall order the words, ONLY YOU CAN PREVENT FORESTS.

In our new age, violence will always end in violence against biology, which gives us a better reason not to make excuses for it. I guess we don't need any external criterion to see the odiousness of what Hitler stood for. But why, with so many external criteria, do we fail to see the odiousness of what we stand for? When black Ron Lockmann was court-martialed for refusing to go to Viet Nam, it turned out that one of the judges had been at Nuremberg; he disqualified himself from sitting. It's not so easy to disqualify the principle of Nuremberg, that we have the responsibility to disobey unjust orders. We must have conducted those proceedings to siphon off a few scapegoats and absolve the rest of Germany, so that we could cooperate with her against Russia. Who guessed then the deadly seriousness of the trial? That, like Oedipus, we pronounced our own banishment from decent society should reinforce our belief in spiritual realities.

It's not that our motives are wholly other than before; but they've got so much more power at their disposal that they seem different in kind. Looking out over the flotsam of Hiroshima or Harlem we may say, "So this is what we intended all along by claiming sovereignty." As population rises we have guided more and more brains into technology, which patches up the air, increases protein production, and crams in more billions of mouths. But sooner or later we'll outreach ourselves; in some area the fabrics of nature and society will begin to rip simultaneously. Our powers to mend will start to fail just where the need is greatest; our complex interdependence will begin to break down. Even now some essential element somewhere not taken account of in all our calculations is approaching the point of exhaustion.

(b) Violence the product of freedom

Our alienation isn't the protest of a detached observer against violence done to a balanced system; rather it's the system itself finding a voice, complaining about what it suffers and assents to. Then if violence has its root in us we can do something about it. Recognition of our role is the beginning of an end to our alienation.

A community where we could start to turn from our violence would be the scene of naturalization. Our primary loyalty would be transferred from where it lies now, in the State, to the group (actual or potential) which we recognized as the place we belonged.

We talk about "unthinking violence," but I doubt if such a thing exists. Consider the areas we have discussed.

(1) No merely natural species can do violence to the environment. Whenever we catch sight of it, it has already multiplied right up to whatever limiting factor prevents it from going further. Violence begins when you see what has put the ceiling over you, and you deliberately supply the scarce item, so that you rise up to the next ceiling, and the next. This requires thought.

(2) The oppression of the poor was taken for granted in the monolithic ancient Near Eastern imperial city; neither they nor their rulers imagined that things might ever be different. Violence could only come out of a new situation where a better way of treating the poor was imagined and rejected by the powerful, who continued to oppress them—but now out of principle, or with a bad conscience, or with the self-persuasion they were doing the best they could.

(3) When classical literatures were being created, every writer treated the language as a businessman today treats the economic system. It was the context he operated in; by mastering it he made his claim to recognition. Only in an age like ours, which through conscious historical study makes an example of older literature, can it be manipulated for propaganda or ostentation.

Thus the idea of violence or exploitation assumes that a natural pattern already exists, and that we take the initiative of choosing more or less consciously to ignore it in favor of something else. *Violence presupposes freedom.*

(c) Freedom as the principle of evolution

The present is the hardest place to recognize freedom. A young man of poor family does well in high school, gets accepted at college, wins scholarships, impresses the interviewer from the defense industry. Freedom? From his point of view it is. But our society needs a lot of people like him, and takes pains to provide them. Undeniable freedom or initiative would consist in discovering an actual new line of action and choosing to take it. How can we tell if a line of action is really new, or a superficial variation on an old theme? The criterion lies in the future, in how the action turns out. Therefore the place to recognize freedom is the *past*, whose future is the present where we're now living.

Now freedom implies something positive: the existence of a fork in the road, even though our knowledge of a man's character makes us morally certain he'll take the wrong way. And when we go back to the freedom which made the wrong choice, a surprise awaits us: *we discover another realm where the right choice was made!* The literary young person finds out with intoxication something his elders hadn't prepared him for: old books contain a deeper intensity of expression than he believed possible. As he grows up, a further discovery is to be made: safe in the past from overthrow by any deathbed folly are revelations of an excellence superior to anything we see around us. No theory could have proved this in advance; it wasn't what the analogy of the sciences would have led us to expect; it just happens to be a fact of experience.

When freedom appears, it has simultaneous effects in two different realms. In one it turns unthinking routine exploitation into conscious violence; in another it produces a fundamentally new level of self-awareness. We recognize freedom in the emergence of some radical novelty into history. The novelty is proved such only by lapse of time, which shows that it can't be dismissed as conformity to a previously existing pattern. Of course the innovator was often deeply aware of being the bearer of the future—with an immediacy which we who look back can't share. But he also had to face the possibility that he might be wrong.

What does it mean to live in a universe where a radical novelty can come into history? At whatever point we approach the human situation we're driven back to this question. Everything around us was once a radical novelty; before then it didn't exist at all. What we mean by history is something new happening. Biological and historical evolution are successive phases of a single process, a sequence of radical novelties. Vegetation was still spreading over the fresh volcanic crater of Lake Nemi when the first King of the

Wood killed his predecessor. The order in which things appeared is built functionally into the present as the way they interlock. Freedom is one of the novelties which have emerged; as it persists in the present, it's the new name for the principle of novelty. For it means that *we* are now responsible for the emergence of novelties in the future.

Man has introduced levels of complexity and order into the universe which could only be actualized in a creature like himself; he has also introduced levels of disorder impossible without his freedom. Can we recognize in the present some radical new reassertion of freedom, comparable in intensity to our alienation? Our analysis suggests that it should be here, but also that it should be here (or in any similar turning point of history) in hidden form. For its emergence can only be recognized by the eye of moral insight; when it can be recognized by its success, it isn't a novelty any longer. To crack open this riddle in the present, we have to go back to the time and place where human freedom first broke through.

I propose as the fundamental turning point the transition from the ancient Near Eastern empires to the free city-state, in both its Hellenic and Hebrew form. The classical city-state was the ostensible pattern for the founders of the American commonwealth. Our contemporary religions in both West and East look for illumination to the same age. Tragedians and novelists go nowhere else for the mythical patterns to serve as the dramatic precedents of their current tales. We shall expect to find that past built as a fundamental layer into our present; when we think about it, we're thinking about ourselves. As we look back there, the irrelevant information we possess about the more recent past drops away; we discover what is in fact essential information.

II

THE EMERGENCE OF FREEDOM AND LOVE IN THE ANCIENT WORLD

1. Knowledge of the human past as centered in the word

(a) The unity and complexity of man in his universe

We gave the provisional name "freedom" to human nature when operating on its proper principles. But no name by itself carries us very deep. We must look for freedom in the monuments of the past. But we also need to set our understanding of man's world and his past against its true background of the larger world and deeper past. The writer or artist must produce a work complex enough to simulate the cross-rips in the tidal waters of being.

Nature uses very grand stage settings, but there's an intelligible proportion between our stature and cosmology. Physical laws ensure that a stable star can't be enormously different in size or heat from our sun. Liquid

D

water and life are only possible within a certain range of temperatures—that is, of planetary distances from a star. Distance by itself determines the length of one primary cycle, the year. Aristarchus of Samos already knew these dimensions. Our own generation has discovered the size of the elementary particles, and conjectured the size of the universe. An intelligent creature needs a brain big enough to contain some minimum number of nerve cells, small enough to be held up against the gravity of a standard planet. All these ratios are built into the original ground plan.

Theory and observation together suggest that the universe is finite and (accurate to a few powers of ten) contains the equivalent of 10^{80} protons. (Eddington's theory—sensational and suspect—identifies the number precisely as $3/2 \times 136 \times 2^{256}$.) These building blocks are grouped in ascending structures:

$$1 \quad \text{gram} = 10^{24} \text{ protons}$$
$$1 \quad \text{star} = 10^{34} \text{ grams} = 10^{58} \text{ protons}$$
$$1 \quad \text{galaxy} = 10^{10} \text{ stars} = 10^{44} \text{ grams} = 10^{68} \text{ protons}$$
$$\text{The universe } 10^{12} \text{ galaxies} = 10^{22} \text{ stars} = 10^{56} \text{ grams} = 10^{80} \text{ protons}$$

If, as seems likely, the universe has been expanding at nearly the speed of light, and its age is ten billion (10^{10}) years, its size is 10^{10} light-years. Most likely it's a hypersphere of finite volume—a three-dimensional orange-peel of curved space twisted round to meet itself with no edges. To visualize the spacing of the galaxies we may roughly think of it as a cube 10^{10} light-years in each dimension. Since the galaxies average a million (10^6) light-years apart, they stack neatly into this cube with ten thousand on a side.

Man is frequently called a little universe or microcosm; we feel our brains in some sense can encompass the universe. These general sentiments may be made more precise. A big man contains 10^5 grams 10^{29} protons. The earth's population is approaching ten billion (10^{10}), or 10^{39} protons. Our individuals are the stars of a small galaxy. If every heavy particle built today into a human being weighed as much as our whole species, the mass of our species would about equal the mass of the universe; we're the square root of the cosmos. A man has perhaps ten billion nerve cells—like our species, he's a galaxy of tiny points of light. The combinations of those cells taken eight at a time would serve to label all the heavy particles in the universe.

Of course these numbers don't get at the unique contents in each irrecoverable instant of our time—whether in our aloneness, in company, or looking at the cosmos. When we asked about freedom, we were looking for nothing less than man himself. To deal with the reality of our instants we need a symbolic record of the happening. Our moment differs from the moment of the animals by its potentiality of generating a permanent record of itself.

(b) Modes of our knowledge of the past

Contemporary reality is stratified: the contents of my filing cabinet are a cross section through time—so is a Near Eastern *tell* or the Grand Canyon. The coin-die of the past leaves its stamp on the present in various ways.

Unaltered deposits of the past. Unchanged fragments of the past—an old Quaker marriage certificate, a Syracusan decadrachm of Arethusa—may come down nearly intact to us, atom for atom. The painted buffaloes and lions of Lascaux open up both the monstrous animal world of the Paleolithic and the archaic mentality that recorded it. Eusebius the Church historian held in his hand the limestone fossil fish of the Lebanon and triumphantly saw proof of Noah's flood. Uranium atoms are a deposit from the original compacting of the earth; their relative abundance (as with the other elements) can be deduced from the sequence of stellar evolution.

Traveling radiation. Most persistent of all are the oldest and least tangible documents of the past—wave trains of radiation. The cosmic hypersphere probably expands from some tight beginning to a maximum and then contracts again. It takes the entire lifetime of the universe for a light ray traveling around a cosmic great circle (which expands and contracts under it during the journey) to reach its starting point again. If our units of space and time are correctly chosen so that the velocity of light is unity, the lifetime of the universe equals its average circumference. The wave trains from quasi-stellar sources ("quasars") or other archaic stellar objects may illustrate a time much closer than ours to the beginning of expansion; that is, they proceed from a place at a considerable angular distance from us around a circumference. Since radiation can't be prevented from traveling, the information it conveys about a different time is necessarily also about a different place. Einstein showed that you can't talk about simultaneity of distant events; further, you can't have certain types of information about the same place at different epochs.

Living communities from the past. We partly understand how an atom maintains itself for millions of years, locked in its crystal; or how a wave train persists, propagated along its geodesic. A colony of horseshoe crabs is just as old, continued in existence by the equally powerful conservatism of self-replacement, which we also partly understand. In the presence of a redwood forest, younger than the crab community, but more massive and more in tune with us, we feel powerfully how an archaic organization of the environment perpetuates itself. Naturally occurring viruses are either survivors or degenerate throwbacks to the original molecules around which the complex unknown chemistry of the primordial sea jelled into life.

The continuity of consciousness. Along the main sequence of evolution we carry monuments of the past around with us in a different way. Our biological development as individuals—begun with the stirring of desire in persons like ourselves—carries us back to as simple a mode of organization as the earliest one-celled creature. Our physical life is correlated with the strangely simple state of affairs called consciousness, something which was always possible in the universe, since it has become actual in us. "Unconsciousness," coma, the sleep of the fertilized ovum, are only cyclic fluctuations in its level. Our part of the world has two sides of its current coin, which Teilhard de Chardin calls the Outside and the Inside: man as the observer with his instruments sees him, and man as he sees himself when observation turns inward. Since we can carry back our personal histories as centers of organization indefinitely deep into the past, our part of the world illustrates every part; every organization of matter and energy must likewise be dual, with some analogues to matter and consciousness, outside and inside.

Primitive man, a Lucretius or Darwin in embryo, correctly saw in the fluid of the womb, as in the water of irrigation-farming, testimony to the emergence of man from the sea. A true instinct led him likewise to locate Gods—centers of cosmic organization—in the animal, vegetable, mineral, aqueous, aerial, stellar worlds. There may be some law of conservation of psychic energy focusing billions of rudimentary insides onto the glowing point of our consciousness. It came as a great surprise that radioactive decay (which at first the Curies found only in radium) was a universal property of nuclei. We can say more: the duality of the universe, at present accessible only in ourselves, must be its most archaic and pervasive property. The fact of consciousness is my key (basically detached from the temporal sequence) to the remote inner sensibility of the beehive or the boiling star. It carries us back to the remotest scene of all, out of which were precipitated the elementary particles and quanta of radiation, as well as the pulsing space-time manifold which envelops them.

(c) Elusiveness of human consciousness in the present

We come closest to catching the psyche in our butterfly net through its relations with other people. The child is licked into humanity by its mother's smiles. During seven years one may have known a lover's body in which the average atom has been once replaced—"this fountain of flesh," Durrell calls it. What is the principle of organization that holds the fountain together, the river we can't step twice in? We're the sum of all that we've known, the area of intersection of innumerable ellipses. The philosopher analyzing perception and knowledge sees consciousness as a baffling simplicity. But in my friend or lover, the consciousness which I can't see generates the character which I can—and it instead has a baffling complexity, inconsistency of successes and failures. If by an effort I try to look at my own self as an outside observer might, dimly I perceive the simplicity and complexity interlocking.

But when I try to fix my mind on my consciousness, after a second or so I realize I'm seeing something else through it; once again the butterfly has escaped. "Consciousness" is the most abstract way of talking about what goes on in my Inside: it's only the invisible atmosphere through which are blown the cumulus of perception, desire, will to power, appetite, curiosity . . . Some of these functions I share more or less with the animals; all (so far as I can tell) have a special color in me. What is that color? My consciousness interlocks with the organization of society around me. My parents were midwife to my self-awareness, and perhaps human society existed prior to individual self-awareness. My consciousness is inseparable from my knowledge of the dimensions of this valley, this planet. Ask the universe where it's aware of its own shape and history, and at that time and place you'll find a man. I hardly dare ask what kind of a universe it can be in which one reaches out for the blueberry on the bush, for the desired object . . .

In the neighborhood of human society, the universe's whole mode of organization is radically changed. How shall we describe the change? If we try to paint a picture of the strictly contemporary world, or write a poem about it, we'll get only mosaic cubes set in a plaster of frustration, anger, desire:

> These fragments I have shored against my ruins.

As the representations of our world become more up-to-date and transitory—a billboard in the corner of our eye, a murder on the television, a cry from the street, a bad trip—we're pushed back into the ungraspable inner chaos we were trying to comprehend. We've been moving in the wrong direction. Art has mirrored life so faithfully that it ends up becoming life, presenting one more problem for itself. We can take that swirling inside world for granted as the raw data of experience to be unlocked; what we still need is a key made of different materials from the data.

(d) Books as central records of the past

Let's go to the opposite extreme and look for the symbolic records of experience which are least contemporary. We can be surest of their permanence by fixing our eye on a past time where more ephemeral records have collapsed—mud walls have fallen and new ones been built on them, marble statues have fed the limekiln, archives have been dispersed, private letters disintegrated in soil or rain, genetic stocks intermingled, languages confounded. Not so far in the past as to go behind the essential features of humanity: the aurochs of Lascaux is mute, it doesn't yet tell us enough, we have to project its society backwards from a better-lit period. We should turn to the precise page where the clear outlines of our society in its most essential features first show up.

Music is what speaks most directly to many of us, the very language of the psyche. For just that reason it eludes our analysis, hard to quote, slippery to interpret. Also it fails us behind the Middle Ages; the music of the Greeks exists mainly as praise of it in their books. The plastic arts cover the whole span of humanity, but are ambiguous where only they testify. Malraux saw in the Nineveh reliefs of the dying lion a pathos absent everywhere else from Assyrian literature and history. I'm not that confident of my eye. Fragments of evidence suggest that the Etruscans were hagridden with superstition; D. H. Lawrence, on the basis of their art, wants to make them blissful pagans. I can't prove my belief that he's wrong. Do the bull frescoes from the Minoan palace of Knossos represent a sophisticated ritual bullfight or a human sacrifice? Where art for the first time, in the archaic *kouroi* of Attica, clearly represents the free man we know, it so happens that its meaning is also defined by contemporary literature; perhaps things couldn't have been otherwise.

What we want to know about the first free men is their understanding of their own society, families, rituals, science, legends—*in their own words*. Here our search comes to an end; the clue to man's past is ancient literary texts. An old book is an unaltered symbolic deposit of the past, preserved through the continuity of consciousness. All the early books had in the first place an oral existence. We can imagine the storyteller repeating the legends of Genesis around the campfire; Plato shows us Ion the Homeric reciter; when Herodotus wanted to "publish" a book of the *Histories*, he rented a stoa and went out to recite it. Not exactly from memory. Our earliest literature is on a knife-edge between oral and written; its technique is oral, but its self-awareness and ambition show that the author was relying also on the permanence of writing. The written text is a mnemonic device to assist the reciter of a text already in principle memorized. The real scene of the text is a sequence of sounds—as heard in the theater, at the festival, in the classroom, on the tape, in the temple.

A sequence of sounds exercises leverage on us through its immensely distant fulcrum in the past, the sea of language that both speaker and hearer swim in. It defines our loyalty to a political idea, freezes the topography of the ocean, assures us of a lover, reconciles or fails to reconcile us to our death. It's not exactly the sounds as such, but the universal ability to classify ranges of variation under thirty or forty categories—the "phonemes" of linguistic theory—that allows so much information, so many overtones, to be transmitted so economically. A real book has a density which provides some kind of equivalent to the crosscurrents of society, the complexity of the nervous system; and at the same time a unity of conception expressing awareness of an organic consciousness. Nothing is more transitory than an utterance as it damps out; but by virtue of individual memories (and writing, the communal memory), nothing is more permanent. Two worm-eaten and faulty manuscripts correct each others' gaps and errors, beat back time's malignant napalm. The phonetic script turns out to be the central symbolic form through which we organize our society, the planet, more than the planet. Ancient history (apart from a few uninscribed monuments) *is* the sum total of the written record, as interpreted by intelligence. For some periods, like those covered by Thucydides and Luke, the basic job of interpretation comes to us already done by ancient intelligence; their text in some sense outranks the events it purports to describe, as an historical event of a higher category in its own right.

Our survey of the past, and our kinds of knowledge about it, led us to ancient books as the scene for the birth of freedom—the basic item in the humanity we know. In an impressionistic survey of ancient history I will suggest that ideographic scripts of the ancient Near East were forgotten in antiquity because they were products of a monolithic sleeping society; that our freedom emerged in the geographical, social, psychic novelty of the city-state, recorded by harmonious texts in alphabetic script; that no sooner did freedom appear than it was corrupted by civil war and exploitation—but only to be transcended by the emergence of an international nonviolent ideology; and that this ideology is the special property of the dispossessed, and the New Testament is their central record. Upon the first basic level of freedom Jesus builds the final second level of love.

2. The ancient Near East and its writing

(a) Phonetic and ideographic scripts

I make a distinction between ancient texts that come down to us in the fully phonetic script of the alphabet (Hebrew, Greek, Latin) and the older scripts that are partly ideographic (Egyptian hieroglyphic and the developments of cuneiform). Knowledge of the ideographic scripts had already disappeared in late antiquity. Egypt and Babylonia lost their self-awareness, and died except so far as they were continued by their daughters—Israel, Hellas, Persia, Islam. But the phonetic scripts are preserved to us by a chain of oral and learned tradition which has worn thin here and there, but never broken. The societies which produced alphabetic texts have influenced later societies, including us, not only because like Egypt and Assyria they were a link in the succession of cultures, but because their texts have been used all along in education.

The complexity of ancient Near Eastern scripts made them a scribal monopoly; they were forgotten when a learned caste didn't consider their preservation important enough to keep itself alive. The simplicity of the alphabet marks a democratization of literature; non-professionals could hand it on. Also the alphabet, by carefully noting phonetic features, both preserved the music of utterance and encouraged writers further in the habit of paying attention to it.

The meaning of all the ancient Near Eastern texts has had to be recovered inductively in modern times. But can poetry which has once died be revived? We're moved at reading a version of the Gilgamesh epic done by a sensitive contemporary; is his pathos really there in the Sumerian? Were those texts composed with the careful attention to music and connotations that we know from modern poetry, the daughter of Greek and Hebrew? Are we sure that the *Book of the Dead* was meant to be read aloud at all?

Egyptian and Babylonian scribes still knew something of their writing for a few generations after Alexander. Why did they let it go? Perhaps their old languages had already been replaced by Coptic and Aramaic, and their script was only a vestigial technique. Then when (if ever) had the texts been living oral poetry? The old religious documents didn't generate reform movements. From behind the veil which no conceivable archaeological discovery could pierce, we conjecture that the priestly class lost interest in the texts because they'd never contained a vital spiritual impulse in the first place. Contrast the Jews, dispersed at several removes from their homeland, who brought their books along in the face of persecution, took pains to preserve a memory of the original tongue, and translated it into their new vernaculars.

A modern who learns the language of Homer or Samuel feels that they go at least as deep into motives and social realities as books of his own language and century. How can he be sure he is not fooling himself? The original pronunciation is defined by beautifully phonetic scripts; we can reconstruct it as closely as the sound of Shakespeare. We have an unbroken chain of commentators. Our spiritual experience is continuous with theirs—precisely because the texts were preserved. We understand their world because it's part of ours, as London abuts on Neolithic farms. We haven't got any of these links to the Near Eastern texts in truly dead languages.

(b) The ancient Near East as monolithic society

The earliest city-cultures appeared in river-valleys, relying not on rain but irrigation. One reason is that, before manuring was understood, a permanent agriculture which could feed on imperial capital required steady replacements of minerals by river-mud. The critical necessity, water, is the key to social structure. The annual rise of the river was the theme equally of engineering and religion. The priests who guaranteed the water by their prayers were colleagues of the civil servants who diverted it onto the fields.

In those valleys, there was no natural acropolis on which an independent community could defend itself against imperial armies; no springs that the defenders of a mound could drink from;

no rain-watered fields to live by in defiance of irrigators. A palace *coup* changed neither the bureaucratic system nor its functionaries. Only once a king, Ikhnaton, formed his own religious notions in the teeth of the hierarchy—and still in the end the hierarchy won out. There wasn't any proud nomadic community to produce an independent thinker; no cult or social institution from which he could get a notion of justice higher than the king's; no simple script accessible to Everyman that his words might be preserved in. A monolithic society: its bread only what the officials licensed, its religion only what the priests did, its law only what the king said.

The first urban cultures had taken so big a step that it paralyzed further initiative. *National Geographic* reconstructions of Nineveh or Karnak look like a more spacious Rome or Cleveland with eccentric architecture and dress. Herodotus, who records his three-day hike into metropolitan Babylon, might not have been surprised by Tokyo. But the ancient city hasn't got any soul: nobody's playing Mozart behind the closed shutters, there aren't any Pentecostal congregations, no hippies practicing Zen, no Communist cells, no universities, no eccentric inventors. We must imagine a world without a free man. Big Brother had to anathematize the nursery rhyme:

Oranges and lemons,
Say the bells of St. Clement's.

But that world hadn't ever heard it in the first place.

(c) Roots of freedom in the ancient Near East

Opposition to arbitrary authority hadn't yet been invented. The workshops made slow technical progress, but nobody thought to sit down and describe the universe. It was religion that motivated the first observation of eclipses, while the great Babylonian astronomers like Kidenas were of the Hellenistic age, and probably touched with Greek rationalism. The ironic detachment of Protagoras' one preserved fragment would have been unthinkable: "Many things prevent us from acquiring accurate information about the Gods; among them, the shortness of man's life and the intrinsic difficulty of the subject."

A scientist friend reports he'd always taken for granted that

Homer and the Old Testament were only the first stumbling steps towards real literature, as unsatisfactory as Aristotle's science in comparison with modern products. How could we affirm what antecedently we'd consider most likely?—there aren't any antecedents to judge by. But it makes us stop and think when the instantaneous eye (trained of course by modern guides) still prefers Greek sculpture of men and women to other sculpture. The struggle of the naked athlete at Olympia or Sparta—as recorded in the statues, praised by Pindar, postulated in the myth of Eden—is a sign of every excellence, "They do it to obtain a corruptible crown, but we an incorruptible." Herodotus modestly is inclined to derive Greek arts from Egypt or Babylon, but still sees that his countrymen have done something new—even though they may never quite have understood what it was. The texts of Egypt and Babylon only came into Greek hands after Alexander, through the Hellenizing priests Berossos of Bel and Manetho; by then the Greeks no longer realized the originality of their own achievements.

Greek and Hebrew literature represent the same men and women as the sculpture, likewise stripped of fetishistic disguises. The Greeks felt sculptors to be mere artisans beside the true maker, the poet; while the Hebrews thought representation of the human figure in any form a blasphemous encroachment on the primacy of the word. They saw the man we see—and for the first time. Had he always been there? But the essence of man isn't merely being somewhere; it is creating a mirror of what he is. Horace says there were great men before Agamemnon, but forgotten because they lacked a sacred bard. Greatness is impossible without a sacred bard; they go together. Between them they constitute a new threshhold in historical evolution; that is to say, in evolution, the unrolling of the world-book.

Every new growth has its roots in what preceded it: life in pre-life, consciousness in the primates. We must look for the roots of freedom in pre-freedom. Where do the old empires dispatch their ambassadors into a potentially more open society? Above all in commerce. The Near Eastern cultures, although their social structure was fossilized, continued to develop technology: domestication, agriculture, metallurgy, mechanics, pre-science. Beyond their frontiers, the empires encouraged the growth of weaker states against the threats posed by each other or by the barbarians. In the second millennium B.C. we see Bronze Age cities outside the empires and not dependent on irrigation. At Syrian Ugarit, Hittite Boghazköy, Cretan Knossos, cracks appear in the monolith. Around these in turn are buffer states—nomadic, or mercantile out of oasis cities, or maritime from fortified ports. Technology spread from Egypt and Mesopotamia through these frontier states, becoming cruder as it went, but still revolutionary enough to produce a demand for its products among the Mediterranean barbarians. The future lay with the traders: Arameans of Syria, Canaanites (including the Hebrews), Cypriotes and Cretans, the people of Anatolia and the Aegean; and then a second generation, Siceliotes, Etruscans and Latins, the Phoenician and Greek colonies.

3. The birth of freedom in the city-state

(a) The citadel as mother of law

How can we describe what it was like when the human race woke up from sleep? The determination to make decisions affecting one's own future; a willingness to be quiet before nature or society and describe it the way it really is; an awareness of new powers of creativity; a fresh look at what had been said of the Gods. Actually, since the new freedom is part of where we stand today, the problem is to understand the sleep of the ancient empires. Our violence, as we saw, is a conscious will to exploitation, different from their habitual petrified injustice.

The decisive step towards self-awareness could only have been taken in a small independent community, what the Greeks called the polis, or city-state—where Jerusalem qualifies equally well as a city-state also. It had to be in touch with older civilizations, but free from outside imperial control, and small enough that a local tyrant couldn't hide behind court ceremonial. These conditions were best satisfied either on an island or an easily defensible acropolis with a natural spring and rain-watered fields. Apparently by

1000 B.C., manuring and crop rotation were practiced widely enough that exhaustion of the soil wasn't a serious problem.

Port-cities for the products of the ancient Near East sprang up on the northern Mediterranean coasts, which are drowned mountain-spurs running into the sea. Especially in periods of Mesopotamian weakness these were relatively safe from conquest by land. The fortified acropolis protected a few acres of ground on which there ruled a law above the will of a tyrant. "The people," said Heraclitus, "must fight for its law as for its wall." And if the wall is lost, all is lost; when "Yahweh determined to lay in ruins the wall of the daughter of Zion . . . her king and princes are among the nations, there is no law" (Lam. 2:8-9).

(b) Iron and the democratic militia

The necessary condition for effective defense of the acropolis was given by the discovery of iron. Another advantage of Canaan was that "its stones are iron." When Odysseus put out Polyphemus' eye with the red-hot stake, it sizzled "as when a bronze-worker [!] dips a huge double-axe or adze in cold water, hissing loudly; and so tempers it, for this is the strength of iron." "Tempers" (*pharmasson*) suggests a secret technique. The Philistines at first kept a monopoly of blacksmithing, and made the Hebrews come down to sharpen their farm tools. So Porsenna the Etruscan—also a foreign exploiting aristocrat related to the Philistines—imposed the condition on the Romans of using iron only in agriculture. But soon the subject locals made the novelty their own, and "beat your plowshares into swords" (Joel 3:10) became the signal for revolt.

Since iron is so much more abundant than copper, not to mention tin, once the secret of its metallurgy had been found, many more men could be armed. The old single combat of an Achilles or Goliath in unwieldy bronze armor was superseded by heavy-armed infantry trained to fight in formation, the phalanx. As soon as ordinary citizens were made the effective military striking arm, they dominated the state, since the citizen militia and the voting assembly were for all practical purposes the same body. Thus during the Peloponnesian War, when the aristocrats of Mytilene against their better judgment armed the lower class, it immediately went over to the Athenians. In a siege (until Assyria developed new techniques) iron seems to have given an advantage to the defense; the Greeks took years to capture cities defended by a few hundred men. Thus the introduction of iron, contemporary with a power vacuum in the Middle East 1200-800 B.C., in two ways had a democratizing effect.

(c) The poet as heir of primitive tribal freedom

It's fashionable to contrast what is called "the Hebrew world-view" with another thing called "the Greek world-view." For our purpose the similarities are more important than the differences. Through movements of people, commerce, institutions, and ideas Greek and Hebrew culture developed in parallel—two foci of a single new emergent. The absence of science and philosophy in Israel is accounted for by the fact that her free state was destroyed before its evolution came full term, and so rational thought was born elsewhere. Greek polytheism and secularism are important but not critical peculiarities, which still do have real equivalents in the Canaanite world. Classical and Hebrew civilization are complementary products of a single spiritual impulse; each is the other's best illustration.

The Hebrews idealized a period when their nomadic ancestors enjoyed complete if primitive democracy. They had before them the example of the Bedouin, independent by virtue of his flocks. Greek legends go back behind the Homeric age (with its well-marked class structure of aristocratic warriors and inferior masses) to a period of dynastic migrations, less clearly defined than in Hebrew tradition, with substantial equality. The technology of the city was essential for the invention of freedom; so also was the memory of that early independence, whether real or imaginary. Awareness of relations with the ancient Near East is expressed in strikingly parallel traditions of emigration; an Abraham and a Cadmus came from the misty east, a Moses and a Danaus (mythical contemporaries) from Egypt. The Hebrews, more radical, envisage the emigration as a general strike; aristocratic Homer is still putting down the uncouth community organizer, Thersites. But in both societies the sacred prophet or bard who recites the traditional account of origins enjoyed substantial immunity from the king or tyrant; he was an enclave of tribal freedom within the city-state.

(d) Freedom and justice in proletarian literature

The origin of the Phoenician alphabet isn't yet understood. The fact that the notion of poetic utterance was discovered simultaneously in Greece and Israel has barely yet been seen as a problem. But it can hardly be an accident that the first use of the alphabet was to record supreme epics of Bronze Age heroes. The introduction of writing was remembered in parallel stories. David sends a letter to Joab by the hand of Uriah (who is either afraid to break the seal or illiterate) commanding the bearer's death. So in the *Iliad*, Proetus sends Bellerophon (surely illiterate) to Lycia, "and gave him baneful signs, scratching [*grapsas*, 'writing'] many destructive things in a folding tablet." Both have woman trouble: Bellerophon like Joseph refuses to lie with Proetus' wife and is accused by her; Uriah refuses to lie with his own wife and so condones her adultery with the king. Uriah is a "Hittite" of Canaan, so here again we may suspect an Anatolian original.

Early poetry was a vocation for the handicapped, a blind Homer or female Deborah, just as smithery was for the lame Hephaestus. It was also appropriate that free literary composition should be the work of the liberated citizen-militiaman or his leader: the verse of a David, Archilochus, or Aeschylus; the prose of a Thucydides or Nehemiah.

As soon as we look outside the acropolis to the circle of agricultural villages which it protects and exploits, we see a new inequality starting to spring up. In the eighth century B.C. we discern in both Greece and Palestine a crisis in land-tenure producing a new class of the poor: originally free farmers who by inefficiency or bad luck went into debt and had to sell themselves, their land, or both, to a class of landlords. We know this because at almost the same time they found a voice in the peasant spokesmen Amos and Hesiod: the first fully realized individuals in world history. It is the Greek who writes, "Make straight your judgments, you gifteating princes," but it might as well have been the Hebrew. Their poetry, almost the first expression of freedom, proves that freedom has already been corrupted.

Both Amos and Hesiod probably lived in an age of literacy. The copiousness of Homeric and Hebrew epic reflects oral style;

the gnomic terseness of the proletarian poets reflects the parsimony of the scribe for whom every line of papyrus was precious. At least they were liberated to tell an unpopular truth like it was, secure in the knowledge that what they had spoken from their hearts would be preserved by their followers through "Phoenician scratchings," *Phoinikeia grammata*.

The farmer-prophet is a radical break from the anonymous courtly singer of epic—doubly so from the scribal functionary of Ugarit or Knossos. He gives its voice to a class that previously had been silent. Both poets talk as if the injustice they condemn was comparatively recent. Both see a principle of justice implicit in the operations of society and the universe. When Anaximander said that things "give each other justice and recompense for injustice according to the order of time," we might have wondered whether he meant the elements of nature or human society. Like us, he sees the balance as being dynamic, whether cyclic or evolutionary.

The essence of freedom is the power of going behind conventions, and seeing principles of order which are superior to human society and guide its evolution. In Chapter IV we'll look at a central feature of the new free society—divine figures and names—and see how they express man's awareness of the new thing which he himself represents, a recently emergent novelty fitting a pre-existent pattern. None of these analyses proves that it was necessary for freedom to emerge at this particular time and place. It's not for us to prescribe beforehand what new thing the universe will next produce. But looking back we can see how environmental conditions—the Mediterranean city-state—both made the novelty possible and gave it a particular coloration.

4. The corruption and transcendence of freedom

(a) The self-destruction of the polis

The splendor of freedom makes us men, driving a four-horse chariot at Olympia in an overflow of symbolic energy, celebrating the victory through choral verse. The same freedom makes violence possible; before too long the Syracusan tyrants monopolized the competition with their stud-farms. The city-state was necessarily ephemeral. Her novelties were adopted by the imperial powers:

E

Assyria and Persia took over alphabetic Aramaic for everything but
ceremonial texts. The advantage of a citizen militia was nullified
by conscription and the invention of siege tactics. A succession of
Mesopotamian powers—Assyria, Babylon, Media, Persia—washed
up against the world of the polis, and captured the Syrian states,
including finally Jerusalem.

Here Greece and Israel diverge; the wave didn't reach Athens
until two generations later, and was enough weakened by distance
that she could resist. In a great burst of energy, Greece (led by the
Syracusan tyrants) secured her independence for another century
and a half; in the same summer of 480 B.C., Pindar noted, she
defeated the Iranian barbarian at Salamis and the allied Car-
thaginian at Himera. In the time gained she worked the logic of
the polis out to the end. Her literature shifted from epic and lyric
to forms not guessed at in Israel: drama, rhetoric, scientific prose
—first history, then philosophy, then natural science. But in the end
she also succumbed to a home-grown imperialism from Macedon.

What went wrong with the polis? When the city-states became
liberated from the ancient Near East, the first thing they did was
fight with each other. Our earliest stories are communiqués of that
war: allied Achaeans against Troy, David against Philistines and
Arameans of Damascus, the growing brutal imperialism of Athens,
the bloodletting of the Peloponnesian War. Nebuchadnezzar and
Philip pushed over states that had reduced each other to shells, and
had almost never stood side by side against the common enemy.

Freedom and violence are twins, from one womb, and the *Iliad*
is a poem of both liberation and force. Antecedently we might have
said that the polis needed only to defend itself. But we're also told
that the best defense is a good offense. Is any offense good? Doesn't
it always overreach itself and fall on its face? The polis consistently
pushed its luck too far. In closely related myths, the Hebrews and
Greeks affirmed that anybody who tries to climb the heavens is
going to get bashed by a power built into the nature of things—
Nemesis, the envy of the Gods, the wrath of God.

Hesiod sees a decline step by step from the Golden Age to the
Age of War, connected with the discovery of iron, and at just about
the right interval before his own time. The Hebrews apparently
project the origin of violence further, onto the first appearance of

man. But by Adam they meant free man, for he wasn't all that many generations before their age, even though the lifetimes were extended to provide a framework for secular history. Eden and the Golden Age are a vision of the possibilities for liberated man, hopefully the mutation we belong to. Greek tragedy remembers a family tree only a few generations behind the new city, and sees the roots of defiant conscious sin as a compulsive repetition of taboos and bloodguilt from the dark past.

Freedom could have grown up, or at least *did* grow up, only behind the walls of the polis. But those walls could only be protected by violence, or at least *were* only so protected. Nothing is easier than to follow the history of that violence from Athens to Saigon. Thucydides is the political philosopher of the human race; Machiavelli and Hobbes are his translators. There's nothing in the mutual suspicions of Washington and Peking which he didn't analyze long ago. The freedom to assert naked man led thinkers to look freely at naked nature—that is, to invent science. Beyond a certain point, science both produces technology and uses technology to advance itself. Then technology becomes autonomous; it was the instrument of violence against society in the ancient world, and against nature as well, in the modern.

(b) Forms of the transcendence of freedom

Violence and its accompanying alienation seems an all but constitutive feature of society. At this point it might be just a play on words to say that the solution was nonviolence. It would be more than that only if something actually emerged in our society or lives which could be so described. But the city-state has a surprise for us; out of that original garden a second bulb starts to bloom. In the death-agonies of the polis various attitudes were possible. Aristotle calmly analyzed what it had been, even as he tutored the pupil who rendered it permanently obsolete. A Demosthenes or Nehemiah tried to patch up its walls when the time for all that had passed. In Plato and Lamentations we read an elegy over its death.

But the poets, with a firmer hold on reality, asked for the meaning of the event, and some of their contemporaries began to work it out in the field of history. Did the death of the polis mean the death of the free man which it had created? No, as it happened, once freedom—like the atomic bomb—had been invented, it couldn't be suppressed. The alphabet couldn't be undiscovered; people persisted in thinking their own thoughts and writing them down. Walls, swords, laws, militia, had originally been needed to make free thought possible. The overwhelming discovery of the fifth century B.C. was that, once freedom had appeared, it could defend itself by new means appropriate to its own nature. Freedom in its original form became obsolete—because it passed into a radically new thing. At the heart of the corrupted city-state, inflicting and suffering violence, was born the image of the free man who affirms his freedom without needing the defense which always turns into offense.

In its first phase the new thing is poetry. At the time of maximum Athenian imperial expansion, Aeschylus set motionless on the stage the figure of Prometheus, of the race of the Gods, suffering for men. He undergoes the Persian punishment of crucifixion— later taken over by the Romans from the Seleucid kings of Syria when they annexed the Near East. (The risen Christ quotes Aeschylus to Paul, "it is hard for thee to kick against the pricks;" Acts 26:14.) Psalm 22, the lament of a forsaken one with pierced hands and feet, represents a similar idealized figure. The Servant poems in Deutero-Isaiah, of the very early Persian period, interpret this suffering: the Servant is Israel; in its dispersion it has the chance of bringing the knowledge of God to the nations. The destruction of Jerusalem is seen as both deserved and providential; Judah must stop being a nation before it can become an international community. Prometheus is blackmailing Zeus by his knowledge that a certain woman will bear a son greater than his father; the Servant has been entrusted with a mission. Both have been let in on a secret: the principle they represent will prevail without the need of propaganda or counter-violence.

(c) The appearance of international communities

The myth is partially realized in the last years of the city-state. In Greece the best representative of the new way is Socrates the hippie with his obnoxious questions at public gatherings. When the State in exasperation finally imprisoned and sentenced him, it also opened a way to escape; he insisted on staying. Jeremiah shows non-resistance to the invader and shares the lot of his people in exile. Israel as a whole, which did things the hard way, fought for her law until the end; but Athens after the war was glad to tear down her walls (the cause of so much suffering) to the music of flute-girls. Out of the death of the city, out of the humiliation of the mythical servant or historical pacifist, a new phenomenon emerges into history: the international community built upon a book.

Plato didn't fully understand Socrates, but through him Socrates lived on in a new idea, the Academy—a community of scholars devoted to a humane literature (beginning with Homer, in spite of Plato's misgivings). The free university, committed only to the truth, so far has weathered persecution; it relies as its adequate defense on the conviction that some people will always respect truth enough to be ashamed of suppressing it altogether. Jeremiah helped found what Deutero-Isaiah is talking about, the Synagogue, another people of a book. Only under the Maccabees and in the modern state of Israel was it in a position to defend itself by force. Normally it just relied on its determination to keep its treasure, the sacred book and its language, alive in the face of persecutions.

These international associations of free men could only have reached maturity behind city walls. But after they grew up there was never quite the same need for the polis again. Nationalism (including Zionism) today is outmoded in the West, the need that originally justified it doesn't exist any longer. (In their cultural lag, Asia, Africa, Latin America are coming to the discovery of freedom through nationalism in a new setting. Our role is to help them through their necessary evolution.) From different beginnings, Synagogue and Academy approached a common task: preserving a canonical literature among the many nations that don't speak its language.

Was it necessary for man to go ahead and commit the violence his freedom made possible? Lower species have built into them the impetus to do everything they can; the first conscious animal seems to repeat their pattern on his level. The Athenians at Melos justified their war-crimes by saying: "Of the Gods we believe, and of men we know, that by a necessary law of their nature they exercise power wherever they can." But they used this principle sophistically. We may explain how a respectable engineer can go on manufacturing napalm by pointing to a widespread pattern of business irresponsibility; but this isn't open as an excuse for the man himself.

(d) The poor as privileged inheritors of freedom

The myths of the Servant and Prometheus have the power of generating fresh life in each age. The first institutions that rose out of them—Synagogue and Academy—have more obvious limitations. Each is a spiritual aristocracy presupposing a long training, mostly literary; they're not for everybody. This limitation fits the general upper-class bias of Greek literature; it goes more against the grain of Israelite culture. But neither institution is comfortable with the agrarian protest of the early poets. What was needed was that the ideology of the aristocratic literary institution should be made available to the illiterate dispossessed: an alliance of the intelligentsia with the proletariat in the service of a nonviolent revolution.

After those original people's poets, the defense of the poor passed from their own number to concerned but paternalistic officials, Solon the magistrate and Jeremiah the priest. Then the poor lost any spokesman, the canon of prophecy was closed. As the Eastern cities passed under the Hellenistic empires and then to Rome, slavery expanded and an urban proletariat appeared. Effective Roman control of the Mediterranean can be pegged at 146 B.C., when she razed to the ground her two commercial rivals, Carthage and Corinth. In 133 B.C. there was a wave of proletarian unrest: a slave-revolt in the Sicilian plantations, a sympathy-strike in the slave-market at Delos, the tribunate of Tiberius Gracchus. The Gracchi were true Marxists, aristocrats taking up the popular cause; but the party struggle they began deteriorated into empty platforms for ambitious generals. There were two more slave revolts before the solidifying of Empire, in 104-1 B.C. in Sicily, and in 73 B.C. at Capua under Spartacus. Thereafter the only revolts of the internal oppressed were the uprisings of Jewish militants in A.D. 68-70 and 135.

As a result the Synagogue went conformist, and a disillusioned Rabbi wrote: "Pray for the peace of the Empire; if it were not for fear of it, each would have swallowed up his neighbor alive." The Academy became an ornament of the bureaucrat's education. Slavery came to terms with the Establishment when Epictetus embraced Stoicism; Hadrian was glad to find his subjects accepting the inevitable. As life in the Imperial state grew ever more arid, the burden of the future came to rest on those liberated by their position at the bottom of the heap from compulsion to cooperate. In corners of the Empire there hung on pockets of a self-conscious agrarian dispossessed, true inheritors of Hesiod and Amos. The normative statement of their position is the Gospels, which Toynbee calls "the epic cycle of the Hellenistic internal proletariat." They were written at a turning point of history—in fact *the* turning point—when free man is willing to dispense radically with the walls and weapons he relied on before. We all understand that Newton, Darwin, and Einstein grasped original insights which will stay valid until the end of time. I propose that Jesus identified himself, both intellectually and also personally, with a new principle that his age was ready for—one that exhausts the meaning of freedom by using it to the end.

5. The New Testament: archive of the dispossessed

(a) The New Testament as a Roman book

Our analysis has led us in front of an old book and asks us to take it seriously. Now that we've gotten so far, let us empty ourselves of preconceptions and make ourselves open for it to speak. What's it about? If we answer quickly that it's about the power of the Spirit, or the Kingdom of God, or forgiveness, or the Resurrection, we show that we haven't heard the question; we've picked up one item of its symbolic vocabulary as if it were a self-explanatory item of ordinary speech. Its title (better translated "New Covenant") marks it as revolutionary. In its own usage that phrase defines the symbolic action of the dispossessed community, "This cup is the new covenant in my blood" (1 Cor. 11:25). Only later on was the name of the action given as title to the archive which interpreted that action; thus it becomes a label of both sacrament and word.

A dossier of documents is suitably called a covenant or charter. It announces a revolutionary transaction arising from the historic situation of its writers. Anybody with something of permanent value to say must say it through his own circumstances; his limitations are the necessary form of his universality. "Strike through the mask," said Ahab. The riddle of the universe assumes one form only for each of us; we deal with it there or nowhere—but if we deal with it there we deal with it everywhere.

The New Testament, like other books, affirms something about the situation, which constitutes its background, and which it can't define explicitly. If an author takes pains to fill us in on certain historical facts, that's part of the story he's telling; his background is the story presupposed at the point where *his* story begins. Is the situation of the New Testament the fulfillment of prophecy? No, that would project the situation into the past; fulfillment is a formal (partly artificial) technique to point up the meaning of the present. Is the situation a waiting for the Kingdom of God? No, that would project it too simply into the future, which for the writers symbolizes the depth of the present. The language of the New Testament is Greek because of what Alexander did, but its situation isn't the fact that the Near East has become Greek. Neither is the situation the Jewish homeland, or dispersion, because its drive is to move out towards a new constituency.

The New Testament is supremely well-written under pressure of an intense urgency. The shifting grammatical forms, oral fragments, tag-ends of phrases, wavering syntax, have the bite and rhythm of life, the compelling tone of men unaccustomed to composition who've been entrusted with something desperately important. If we want a single adjective for the situation, we must say that the New Testament is a *Roman* book, a response to the radically new state of affairs produced by the founding of the Empire in 27 B.C. The book which comes nearest to having the same situation is the *Aeneid*, although it says something quite different about it. The situation of the New Testament is the problem presented to the individual and the voluntary community by a state which arrogates all meaning for itself, the problem of alienation from natural roots produced by Establishment violence. Vergil, with subtle doubts, on the whole accepts the Empire's self-evaluation. The revolutionary or "New" side of the New Testament announces resistance to Empire; the "Testament" part defines the nature of that resistance.

The surface layer of Romanization is Latin words that have been naturalized into New Testament Greek, and often also into an underlying Aramaic. The following list could be expanded from early Christian literature: *mile, libra* ("pound"), *modius* ("bushel-basket"), *denarius, assarius* ("penny"), *quadrans* ("farthing"), *linteum* ("towel"), *sudarium* ("face-cloth"), *paenula* ("cloak"), *macellum* ("market"), *census, colony, sicarius* ("assassin"), *libertinus* ("freedman"), *custody, flagellate, speculator* ("executioner"), *title* (on the Cross), *centurion, praetorium, legion, triumph.* That so much of this vocabulary needs no translation shows how far the Romans have imposed on us also; its exploitative imperialist stamp, at once metric, economic, political, and military needs no underlining. And it's only a superficial stratum of Roman influence, since the Greek cities had long before invented chaste Attic equivalents for the really important official vocabulary of *proconsul* and the like.

Palestine was occupied territory. Against the alleged threat of infiltration from the desert by raiding bands or Parthian armies, a foreign military usurper had called in the Western imperialist power. Its professional troops were quartered on the countryside by a puppet administration whose dynastic rivalries show how little popular base it enjoyed, and which was frequently bypassed by the commanding general. The native prelate had to apply in person on holy days for his vestments, which were locked up in a fortified consulate and issued only to the approved tenant of his office. The liberal intellectuals, ostensibly modernizing traditional customs and religion for relevance to contemporary needs, were in fact a conservative force; the colonial power, by granting them modest perquisites, had detached them from any revolutionary movement. Those obsessive figures of popular literature, the absentee landlords, were obviously (along with their resident stewards) reliable

supporters of the regime which suppressed insurrection. Undoubt-
edly they found ways to recoup from day laborer and consumer the
protection money they paid—an inflation of 500 percent per century is recorded. No one but the foreign non-coms can have been
the regular clients of the prostitutes omnipresent in our sources.
The roster of colonial agents is completed by the locally recruited
orderlies of the foreign officers, and the universally unpopular outcasts who collected taxes for corporations capitalized overseas.

(b) Jesus and the Galilean Resistance

The explicit pages of Josephus, and the writing between the
lines of the Gospels, show that the rural North was the breeding
ground of a fanatical patriotic Resistance under Messianic claim-
ants. The massive uprising sparked off by Nero's approaching fall
in A.D. 68 implies a long line of predecessors. Several of the Apostles were named by their fathers after Maccabean freedom fighters:
two Simons, two Mattathiases, two Judases, at least one John. One
is explicitly a "Zealot," two are "sons of thunder" who would like
to call down fire from the sky. All are looking for an anointed king,
legitimated by descent from David; one Simon thought to have
found him, and is disaffected when told that this one won't triumph
as the world judges. So at a desert caucus the proposal is made to
"take him by force and make him king"—the drafting of a reluctant
Presidential candidate. A famous saying of the proletarian organizer Tiberius Gracchus is put on his lips: "The beasts that inhabit
Italy have their den, but those who fight and die for Italy wander
homeless and unsettled with their wives and children." Galilee is
the impregnable stronghold of a National Liberation Front, the
water that its fish swim in—impregnable because the counter-insurgency forces could never locate any resistance to put down. The
Twelve Apostles were born Viet Cong. The liberation movement
had a less stable urban base; if we changed the scene a little we
could define the rebels put down by Titus the law-and-order Man
as Black Power militants.

Jesus isn't identical with Galilee; but the New Testament betrays its Resistance origins by engaging in polemic with the claims
of the Emperor, sometimes openly, at all places covertly. Beelzebul

"Lord of the Mansion" and other demonic powers are seen to have infiltrated the power-structure; "My name is Legion." Paul formally recognizes Caesar's authority, but slips into revealing his conviction that the Lord of glory was crucified by the "magistrates (*archontes*) of this eon" (1 Cor. 2:8).

Conversely imperial titles are heaped on Jesus; for generations before him official cult had praised the Emperor as "Savior," spoken of the *evangel* of his birth, welcomed his Advent (*parousia*) into the provinces. John knows that Domitian wished to be called "Lord and God" and pointedly transfers the phrase to Jesus. The Emperor spared Italians the indignity of having a king (*rex*) over them, but was addressed as *basileus* in the Greek East—or by an Achaemenid Persian title, "King of Kings." "Christ" itself was the native regal title, disavowed by Jesus in his lifetime, and bestowed on him by the Hellenistic Church.

We'll do well not to try to prove that Jesus had to be born in a certain time and place. But since we know that in fact he was born, we'll understand him better—or transfer the mystery in him to where it belongs—by studying that time and place. His geographical base was the Galilean insurgency, its members rejected as a profane miscegenated caste by both the clergy and the liberal intellectuals ("Pharisees"). The Fourth Gospel must be theoretical reconstruction in having Jesus make all those trips to the occupied capital, for the erratic urban mob can't ever have stood firmly behind the rustic folksinger of nonviolence. In large part the potentially guerrilla countryside had been organized by an ascetical reformer, thought to be a relative of Jesus, John "the Baptizer." Both his origins in the South and his attitudes link him with the Essene monks of Qumran, who also were "preparing the way of Yahweh in the wilderness."

Neither Jesus nor the Palestinian Church disavowed those origins, for they took as their symbol of initiation John's washing of rebirth. Jesus uses the metaphor of baptism in his own words while not urging the act on his followers; after his death, however, the Twelve do urge it. The obvious conclusion is that they, and the rest of his following, came to him through John's baptism. For Jesus then the community of John *is* Israel; it's what he starts from, and in part disagrees with. Besides his decisive break with violence, he breaks also with John's asceticism. He must have regarded the shift as important, while recognizing that it wasn't any more acceptable to the cynical uncommitted. "John came, not eating and drinking, and they said, 'He has a demon'; the Son of Man came eating and drinking, and they said 'A glutton and winebibber, the friend of whores and collaborators.' "

(c) The new community as Liberated Zone of love

New Testament scholars, in an excess of Establishment scrupulosity, make difficulties about the authenticity of many items in the Gospels. Our present line undercuts these doubts: the Roman background of the New Testament stands absolutely firm. These documents bear on their face the genuineness of what they claim to be: the record of a counter-Establishment community of the dispossessed. Equally clear is the question the New Testament is asking in its Roman situation: How can authentic community exist and spread in an exploitative society?

If we take the Gospel at face value, there won't be any doubt how to answer this question. New Testament scholars hesitate to take the Gospel at face value—because it's a deposit of oral tradition and legend, because they're afraid to. It's true we haven't got the same kind of history here that we've got about Cicero; but who ever wanted to throw in his lot with Cicero? Academic historiography is set up to define the records of official literary persons as valid, and the records of popular nonliterary persons as invalid. This accurately reflects Establishment defensiveness in the face of revolutionary threats. Rather than doubt the validity of the attitude toward exploitation ascribed to Jesus, we should doubt the validity of our own attitude to exploitation.

We may say very simply that if Jesus followed the right kind of course, the knowledge that we possess about him must be the right kind of knowledge. He trusted that a popular oral tradition wouldn't falsify anything of critical importance that he stood for— but rather was the best or only way to preserve it. This gives us a new clue which things are of critical importance. We love the memories of men like Socrates and Francis who take pains not to impose themselves on the future, but throw themselves on its mercy. (We can't feel the same way about Dante, who invented a rhyme scheme from which no verse could be lost without detection.) Love written down is legend. And in combination with other kinds of evidence, legend is our best or only proof that a special kind of man has lived.

Old Khrushchev, hitting the table with his shoe, knew what manner of man Jesus was: "If someone hits you Christians on one cheek, you turn the other cheek; if someone hits us Russians on one cheek, we hit his cheek so hard we knock his teeth out." The beautiful outsiders who are boycotting the Church for not being like Jesus have a clear picture what he was like. One rejects the Church of Jesus for pretending to follow him; the other rejects it for not following him. Both see it as it is, and know him as he was.

What he was may be thought of as a permanent sortie from the citadel of freedom, *the Liberated Zone of love.* Jesus doesn't propose that something new should happen in the future; he announces that it is currently happening in the midst of men. He calls the attention of his audience to the fact that, without their having noticed it, a new flower has grown out of their soil. Actually he has several audiences, and an appropriate message for each. For hostile questioners from the authorities he has the barbed answers of controversy: "I came not to call righteous but sinners"; "He is not the God of the dead but of the living." For the curious he has the parables, where he appears to divest himself of his own principles, and shows that the new way follows even from the convictions of the children of this age. For the committed, those who become his movement, or rather whose movement he becomes, he tells it like it is.

We've seen how he accepts and transforms his geographical base of organized fanatic revolutionaries. His ideological base is liberal Pharisaism, the thing which he starts from and rejects the most decisively—because he knew it was the stance that his movement would most likely fall back into again. His personal base is the women and pietists whom he radicalizes at the same time he humanizes the ascetics, strips their violence from the insurgents, and deflates the intellectuals. Each element is turned upside down, the last becomes first, the least becomes greatest.

He turns inside out a community already existent. In what was remembered as his initial manifesto he redefines that community: for he found it at once (1) *hesitant about its role*, and (2) *hasty in action*. We're so familiar with the text that we need an effort of imagination to recapture the original mixed emotions he elicited, for he was pushing his hearers in two directions at once.

(d) The tree and its fruits

(1) "Blessed are you poor; for yours is the kingdom of God." *They were hesitant about their role*. The dispossessed community needed to be given a name, to be held up to its own best insights. They'd been taught to look for a coming state of affairs when the Liberated Zone of God's sovereignty would be plainly operative. Normally in Judaism—above all in Jesus' Viet Cong circles—it was assumed that the Kingdom would be brought in by a legitimate descendant of David, a royal Messiah (and with violence). But the early chapters of Luke point to a community of pious among the dispossessed which was groping to see itself as the bearer of the Kingdom (and without violence). The Magnificat, which probably belongs to Elizabeth, mother of the Baptizer, takes up the song of Hannah: "He hath filled the hungry with good things, and the rich he hath sent empty away."

Jesus states it as a fact in the Beatitudes that the hungry are filled with good things. What made it a fact? That he said it with antecedent authority? But our evidence (or the evidence of his first hearers) for his authority springs from what he was. And it's a man's words which define what he is—since our words crown the whole symbolic language of gesture and bearing. Or was it a fact in the sense that Jesus found the blessedness of the poor already existent? But it wouldn't have existed effectually without him (or somebody like him) to define and guide it. Our language breaks down when we try to explain how a new thing is born. We may say: Jesus found the Messianic community existing potentially among the dispossessed, and by recognizing it as such made it actual.

What made him so sure the right kind of community was there? He had the history of Israel going for him, where inheritance, contrary to precedent, went through the younger son, the harlot, the foreigner of goodwill. The figure of the Servant of Yahweh defined a dogma that truth would be internationalized through a suffering community. The circles symbolized by Mary, Elizabeth, Simeon, Anna, Zacharias, had been brooding over the prophecy.

Political revolutionaries saw a promise to the poor in contemporary history. Toynbee shows that the idea of a proletarian revolution led by converted aristocrats was in the wind—Agis and Cleomenes in Sparta, the Gracchi in Rome. Marx's analysis of ancient history wasn't arbitrary; he takes as normative the categories and vocabulary in which the ancient historians had previously analyzed it.

Detroit or Hanoi or Guatemala are examples of how a submerged community may suddenly become conscious of its identity and power. Various things may precipitate the revolution—sometimes when an imperialist power feels a touch of guilt and grants paternalistic concessions. That consciousness is abroad in the world today, as it was in the first century, and in the radical Protestant reformers of the sixteenth. Jesus' political friends turn out to have been wrong; they would necessarily be obliterated by the Imperial armies. Jesus makes a virtue—the only virtue—out of that necessity. The revolutionaries, including the Twelve Apostles, were going about things in the wrong way. But before Jesus can say so, he has to reassure the dispossessed as radically as possible that they are the bearers of the sovereignty, that the new emergent has surfaced in them; they are the new (in some sense final) bud on the world-tree.

(2) "But I say to you who are listening: Love your enemies." He's not saying this to the rich—who have just been denounced and evidently aren't on the scene—but to the present poor. And he tells them that they'd been *hasty in action*, they'd jumped to conclusions about the way their Messianic role would be exercised. The normal Messiah, after (one may presume) assuring his hearers that they're destined for a key role in God's plan, then issues the call for the sword. "Baby, get yourself a gun." The Apostles began to fink out, whether they realized it or not, when finally they came to see that he meant what he said about the sword. That doesn't alter the fact that he maintains solidarity to the death with their cry against injustice, and they knew it. And in the end it turned

out that they'd heard him too well to go back to violence, and one by one after his death they sheepishly returned.

The new imperative, *Love your enemies*, doesn't really go beyond the Beatitude, *Blessed are you poor*. For how could he be so sure they were blessed? Because he had the insight—the final discovery by the cosmos of the principles defining its own existence —that the true pattern of life was the nonviolence which the poor were already practicing. Some were practicing it only for the time being, in frustrated impotence to take the sword; others because they'd begun to see it was the right thing. Jesus must have been the child of some community, or there wouldn't have been anybody to hear him; he truly calls the community his mother, and teaches it the true meaning of what he learned from it. Their blessedness lies in the fact that even as they listen to him they become what in principle they already were. The Kingdom of God is self-realizing; it consists in people recognizing that it's already happened. As the human community is the universe become conscious of itself, Jesus is the human community become conscious of itself. Their consciousness consists in taking on their shoulders the new kind of freedom born from the death of the polis. But they didn't so much take it on their shoulders as have it put on them, and it's more than a higher freedom. Better to say: they accepted from history the burden of love.

Who or what is Jesus himself in relation to the community of the dispossessed, which he has asked to see itself as bearer of the Kingdom? His person is unimportant beside his message: "Why do you call me Sir, Sir, and don't do the things that I say?" Still of course it's he that says it and not somebody else. If there's one thing that emerges with complete certainty from the Gospels, it's a massive consistency in Jesus' character. Everything fits together— without the strain we feel in St. Paul or ourselves. His actions illustrate his words—as they should, since words are symbolic actions. But who else has spoken without an element of self-condemnation? All the rest of us are Oedipus. Jesus has some claim to be an authority on words; more exactly, he *is* word. The man himself, in both action and suffering (which add up to refusing to be the Messiah), is what he advocates. The Mediator is the message.

Still in his truthfulness he must also deal with the fact that the new way has come through him and not through somebody else. "If I by the finger of God cast out demons, then no doubt the kingdom of God has come upon you"; "You have heard that it was said to them of old time. . . ; but I say unto you . . ."; "Whoever confesses me before men, the son of man will confess him before the angels of God." He's passed through to the other side both of pride and humility. The new principle of humanity—or rather the principle by which humanity is to be constituted for the first time —has been incarnated in him. In the end the principle takes precedence; his person is unimportant beside his message, precisely because the message is one of non-self-assertion. "I am in the midst of you as one that serveth"; "The Son of Man hath not where to lay his head." The more he points to his own role as representative of new humanity, the more he recedes into the background. "As the lightning shines from one horizon to the other, so shall the son of man be in his day; but first he must suffer many things and be rejected by this generation" (Luke 17:24-25).

When he talks about the "son of man," he doesn't mean clearly either himself or the community; but rather the community as reconstituted around the principle which he illustrates. Even Caesar felt obscurely that it was inexpedient to be called "King." The kings of the nations lord it over them; their great ones are called benefactors, but in the community the greatest are those who wait on table. He who humbles himself shall be exalted; Jesus states this as a general principle, which the Church then sees illustrated in him above all.

(e) Initial problems with the new way

After the execution of Jesus, an activist theoretician discovered another class of oppressed poor in the miscegenated ghettos of the Mediterranean port-cities. Paul's letters translate the rural metaphors of Jesus into the idiom of those stevedores, semi-reformed prostitutes, marginal businessmen, small-scale artisans, unstable enthusiasts, slaves and freedmen, tavern-keepers, petty collaborators, faithful human beings. The center of gravity has shifted in the New Testament Epistles, but still to our surprise we

F

hear the very words of Jesus worked into the apostle's exhortation: "If you suffer on account of righteousness you are happy" (1 Peter 3:14); "Bless your persecutors and don't curse them" (Rom. 12:14). For three centuries, persecution kept the Christian Church willy-nilly loyal to nonviolence. But at subsequent periods of Church history, at least two objections have been felt to Jesus' program: (1) that he did not practice it himself; and (2) that it's impracticable.

(1) Is the person who doesn't see things our way the enemy we're meant to love? Jesus doesn't seem very loving to one group at least of those who disagree with him: the Pharisees. Two other groups present easier problems. Some on our side openly advocate violence to overthrow injustice. In a sense the Galilean Resistance is his enemy, for it betrays him; but he expresses solidarity with its struggle for justice, while trying to humanize it. There are those on the other side who openly exercise violence to maintain injustice in power: the Romans. These are the enemy, properly speaking, that his sayings apply to.

The Pharisees are those on our side who tacitly benefit from injustice. We agree that Jesus ought to have denounced them as he did; the problem is in finding a way to love them. They aren't exactly the enemy. "And therefore they don't deserve to be loved? What is this advantage that our enemy has over our friends?" The advantage of not purporting to speak for us; we don't have to reject the claim that he's representing our viewpoint. Loyalties and group memberships are illegitimate extensions of our personality; through them we can push other people around by our agents without having to take the blame ourselves. We should take pains to dissociate ourselves from injustice allegedly done on our behalf; with the actual enemy the situation doesn't arise. When analyzed through to the end, the notion of "enemy" is contradictory; Jesus is such a thorough philosopher that he can't bear the dilemma, and so deals the enemy out of existence.

People ostensibly on our side who represent injustice are also people in their own right. If we can pass beyond ideology, there's a clear alternative of their becoming actual enemies or actual friends. The presence of Jesus polarizes people into making decisions. He takes maximum risk himself in getting as close as possible to the other person's position, maintaining solidarity with error. In the story of the Prodigal Son he assumes all the criticisms of the Galilean outcasts to be true—and shows that even so they deserve forgiveness. He presumes that from every point of view there's some road leading to the truth.

He's more severe on the class than on individuals. To make a distinction between a man and his erroneous views, the ancient world had something more powerful than we do; it had demons. It could retain respect for a man who is in the wrong more easily than we can; it could say he was serving the wrong master, whereas we doubt if there are any masters to serve. So the apostle can maintain that the Emperor holds his power from God, and still recognize that our battle is against spiritual wickedness in high places. Behind the man Caesar and his providential office is his Genius, a demonic power which has subverted the Government. The Beast of the Apocalypse issuing Social Security numbers and draft cards to those who recognize its authority symbolizes this reality concretely. If we agree that the Beatitudes define the human ideal, how can we retain respect for our fellow human beings (ourselves included) unless we can find a way to say that they're gripped by some demonic possession—alcoholism, fetishism, lust for power, self-justification?

It's easier when the demon attacks the oppressed and makes them outcast; they're still accessible to our compassion. But what shall we do when such a one holds supreme power? He's cut off from us; the demon's got him where it wants him. The top and bottom of society, Presidency and Bowery, are subject to the same compulsions: the great advantage of the poor, which helps make them blessed, is that they can't provide the demon enough power to shut off a healer's access.

(2) It's been said that society can't be conducted on the basis suggested by the words of Jesus, and that we shouldn't pretend it can. But history has put the shoe on the other foot. For it seems now that society can't be conducted much longer on the basis of our current level of violence, and the Church shouldn't pretend that it can. People who try to follow neither doctrine treat what Jesus says about violence and hatred as if it were the same as what he

says about using the courts or saving money. If "take no thought for the morrow," "sell what you have and give to the poor," can be understood metaphorically, then why shouldn't "turn the other cheek," "love your enemies" be taken in the same way?

We know that prudence and an income aren't intrinsically bad, as are hatred and killing. Therefore the first kind of saying must be interpreted along different lines from the second—though I suppose as seriously. Since we die tomorrow, we're not supposed to be anxious about it, but do the best we can today. Food and security are those items which we shouldn't necessarily claim for ourselves, but which (being good) we're expected to provide for others. But violence isn't something we give up so that others may enjoy it in our place.

(f) The birth of Aphrodite

To one side of us the Gospel comes as something external and threatening. To another side (hopefully dominant) it comes as a fresh breath out of our own life, an almost forgotten morning of our own childhood. In this world of violence we find ourselves chucked into, the noisy reassertion of the polis in the bigger and less responsible form of the Nation doesn't seem to offer any way out. Over against all the voices assuring us that the Gospel says something more complicated and compromised than it appears to, we'd like to affirm that its way is what it says, and that it's *our* way —the Ariadne's thread of nonviolence which alone offers to lead us out of the maze, turning our back at every point on the Minotaur of conscious bestiality.

The wreath promised at close of day for having held to the right course is simply survival: for the planet, for society, for ourselves. The initiative lies with us. Jesus suggests, and our heart seconds his motion, that the key which will unlock the collectivities must first unlock us. More truly than any president of General Motors, we may say, "If it's good for us, it's good for the nation."

In the next chapter we'll try to ask if the Gospel is something more than a grammatical fiction, if nonviolence really exists. It appears that our philosophers have been doing bad metaphysics, and our political scientists, bad community organization. The true contents of our psyche isn't consciousness: either in its origins, since it came from our mother; or in its goal, since it was intended to reach out for the desired object. The true principle of our social organization isn't freedom, which can only oscillate between defense and attack, isolation and imperialism. The message which comes in from alphabetic texts, from the farthest reaches of time and space (mediated through our self-awareness), unifying all literary forms, dissolving the threat from the astronomic dimension of things, resolving the dilemma of society, is simply love.

Since Greek religion hasn't got any priestly guardians of orthodoxy, we're entitled to pick and choose among its themes. And I guess if we thought about it most of us probably would choose the birth of Aphrodite, purified of gross Phoenician motifs, perfected by Botticelli's innocent version of the naked figure on her scallop-shell in the foam. The Gospel purports to offer us nothing less than we ask for, the birth of love; before we let the realists whittle the gift down to their size, we might first see how it looks when we open the package.

III
REVOLUTIONARY NONVIOLENCE

1. The demands of justice and love

(a) Identification with the oppressed

The historical fact that Jesus identified himself with the oppressed also makes a claim on us. Establishment political theory takes membership in "our" society as simply a given fact; but the claim of the poor, however little we respond to it in practice, has higher priority. We already suffer along with them at pauperization of the environment, both biological and spiritual. Solidarity demands conversion, so far as we're now identified with the exploitative society. We must begin to think not "our violence" but "their violence," not "their suffering" but "our suffering."

How shall we work effectively against current violence, without starting a new chain of violence? Many who've gotten this far consider the dilemma insoluble, and settle for either ineffectiveness or counter-violence. We have to reject both alternatives.

Establishment nonviolence. Respectable pacifism is novocaine to deaden our awareness of complicity; it's the Establishment's ultimate technique for castrating our resistance. When I cash in monthly dividends from past violence how can I be called nonviolent?

Revolutionary counter-violence. The cry

of the oppressed for forcible revolution is a necessary feature of the cry for justice. But if we refugees from the Establishment echo it uncritically, we won't be serving either morality or the future. The adherence of intellectuals should at once vindicate and transform the struggle of the poor. We can't just set colored people in the chairs of power now occupied by the colorless, to make the same mistakes all over again. History has moved and they've got to do better than we did.

The third way, recommended by the Gospel and our necessities, is *revolutionary nonviolence*. Ethics refuses to accept a choice between two evils as exhausting the possibilities. Novelties come into being by openness to a creative alternative. Of course at the same time nothing is more risky; this waiting is only the thickness of a razor blade from the shiftlessness that sinks back into conventionality.

(b) The demands of justice on its two levels

Solidarity with the victims of injustice implies some idea what justice would be like.

The level of absolute individual rights. Justice is the state of affairs where every man has his place in the sun, and every woman and their kids too; and shelter if the sun gets too hot and against rain. Clothes for use and to define a respected position in society. Foods in season and some out of season, frozen or imported. A bed to sleep and make love in. Symbolic ancestral possessions (not necessarily money or land) and things of one's own; a place to keep them and the kids' toys. A skill if possible of one's own choice, and a job to use it at. A clean beach to swim from, mountains to climb in. A dignified way of getting the doctor. Freedom not to have the kids arbitrarily interfered with. Freedom to travel, freedom to assemble with people of the same background or a different one, freedom to read, listen, look. Freedom to sound off and make a fool of yourself—or maybe a wise man. Freedom to go on speaking the language your mother taught you.

The package presupposes justice towards tame animals, the right of most wild animals and plants to exist—the sympathetic management of the planet. Absolute justice won't be realized until the Garden of Eden sets in—all the more important then to start working towards it. The item most critically lacking at any moment, food or freedom, will be what justice demands; but people must set their own priorities.

It's our duty to insist on all these things for our neighbor. Our own discovery of the Gospel puts matters in a different light for us (potentially for him too). If we now enjoy these freedoms, by a higher principle than justice we (like other revolutionaries) may renounce them for ourselves to guarantee them for him. But no one is in a position to make that renunciation for somebody else, except by setting the example.

The level of relative rights. It would be wrong to say that justice was *giving* every man his place in the sun. If some administrators give him that place, they can take it away again. But it must be arranged that the right goods and services are produced, that people don't make more new people than the planet has convenient niches for, that people don't need to fear aggression. The second level of justice is the relative right to existence of institutions which defend the absolute rights.

The language that defines our freedom binds us into primary communities—the people around us who speak our mother tongue. Any threat to that community attacks us as individuals. The myth of Babel sees different languages as the typical failure in communication which generates hostility. The myth of Pentecost envisages the hope of breaking down that barrier through simultaneous translation technique. If something important has already been said in our language, or if we can say it ourselves, the linguistic community is guaranteed by its own proper means.

Relying on the wrong sort of guarantee is the scene of corruption. In our suspicion of our neighbor (often well-justified, always self-fulfilling) we seek out or cling to collectivities—a Church, a cultural group, a city, a nation, a legal system—as embodying our primary rights. But no polis or Establishment is entitled to claim identity with our rights, even when people have invested their life in it.

If the institution is big and faraway, it must be stable enough to base my plans on, but also flexible enough that under social change it won't go on enforcing what would then be injustice. That's difficult. So all arrangements should be guaranteed on as local a level as possible. Locals are best acquainted with their own situation. Only rare people are wiser than their neighbor at recognizing his needs. Wherever possible *people are to make decisions affecting their own future.* The closer to home a system of self-defense, the more modest its claims will be, for it sees its own temptations. The justice of an institution varies inversely with its claim to justice.

(c) The demands of love in an unjust society

For the man who has everything, Jesus makes only one gift suggestion, "Sell what you have and give to the poor": identification with the oppressed. Otherwise his message is to the oppressed —who now of course ideally include the former rich man. In a unified world with some prosperous communities, the poor are victims of injustice simply by existing. There's always an area where men could start restoring justice if they wanted to badly enough.

It's always phony when big people accuse little people of crime. The powerful can't be victims of injustice; they haven't got any enemy except Death. The rich who hold power by keeping the poor ignorant and divided do have another enemy, whose name is Revolution. They must make their own judgment whether it's inevitable. We should help them make the decision to start unloading their cargo of injustice. Otherwise we can only say, "Woe to you rich, for you already have your reward." Their placid exercise of injustice has weakened their psyche, and the revolutionary poor rush into the psychic vacuum.

The only war worth taking sides on is the refusal of the oppressed to accept further exploitation. If we're in their shoes, for the first time we can locate an actual enemy and think about loving him; that is, the Gospel becomes applicable. When a big power fights a little power, one party has an enemy; the other party has only a victim. If the revolution succeeds, as it eventually will, the roles may be changed. That doesn't affect the current state of affairs, but it explains why Jesus forbids military identification.

Jesus, who takes the cry against injustice for granted, finds a new basis for solidarity among family and friends in a higher solidarity with the enemy. But even in his name we can't ask the apathetic peon to love the man sitting in the hacienda, until he's realized that he's got an enemy and revolution is possible. Only then will it be a real decision, and not a formula, for him to transform the revolution into nonviolence. Since in some sense it's always possible to love the enemy, the revolution as Jesus transforms it can always be carried out. Love is more practicable than justice. This is why he can be so sure that the poor are already bearers of the Kingdom.

Love of the enemy is recognition of the fact that the evil doesn't lie in him but in demonically controlled structures. As we, with no special merits or insight, have gone over from the occupied territory into the liberated zone, so can he. He's hostile to us because we reinforce the reality-principle in him which tells him the truth about the Establishment he belongs to. As he constantly stands before a fork in the road, our job is to keep recommending the right way.

The emerging nations are only approaching the stage where the Greek city-state discovered itself, and we've got to let them evolve from the point they've reached. We can't disavow *our* history either; we've passed beyond that point. We're most securely anchored in the two terminal points of evolution—nature and the Gospel. So long as the biological environment holds up, we needn't fear for the Gospel from violence (the background it was born in) but only from compromise.

This chapter works out the basic alternatives which persuade me that the only way to work for peace is peace. The coercion available to a Great Power today—ostensibly in the service of justice—is deployed on two levels, with a big gap in between. We'll fight either against a little opponent, with limited means, exercising what we may call police power; or against an opponent we choose to consider as equal, with unlimited means, in what is still called by the old name "war." The policy of force is then shown to be bankrupt by a clear dilemma. That doesn't mean that the State (a passive agent under demonic momentum) will necessarily drop the policy; but that as individuals we must find another line of constructive action.

A war against a small opponent, like other exercises of police power, will turn out in the end to have been neo-colonialist. It will be unjust and undermine our society; therefore it won't work. True police power works best where it's least needed. On the other hand, a war against an equal opponent involves the unavoidable risk of damaging the biological environment. Nothing can justify this risk; for the Gospel is available in seed-form around the world. This prudential nonviolence seems different from the New Testament motive of eschatology. But in fact the apocalyptic vision was a true prophecy of the threat in technology. The hard case of nonviolence —the one where Jesus originally recommended it—is in a just people's revolution. Our cue is to show the revolutionary here or overseas that he'll eventually win, and should start off on a better foot than we did. This message is our permanent service. The scene of our effectiveness isn't the police power of the State, but the voluntary community of love.

2. False and true police power

(a) The levels of police power

My New Hampshire college town had a paid three-man police force which directed traffic and issued bicycle licenses on Saturday mornings. Every October the students decided to raid the movie theater; once the police were reputed to have thrown a tear-gas bomb. I suppose anybody with sterling locked the house up when they went out, but we didn't know anybody like that. Every transient was spotted the day he hit town. A couple of summer drifters slept in shacks beside their rowboats on the river.

Our local uptight Puritanism—the serpent in this granite Eden —produced neuroses, and drunkenness after Repeal. Even in Nashua and Manchester the Canucks and Irish were only a marginally oppressed class—our situation was pretty different from the South. How far was our relative harmony parasitic on the original institution of slavery, funneling profits to the industrial North? We didn't see too much of them. Only when the black ghetto starts spreading up through Lawrence and Lowell will we know we've joined the twentieth century.

Our current suburb regulates itself by a similar vigilante code of morals. My neighbors work off anti-social impulses in their cars and hire traffic cops to protect them from their own frustrations. What are all those other police—that we get taxed for—doing? Some petty racketeers in bookmaking, pushing, prostitution, protection, are picked up; the big boys are in the Mafia, whose base is its infiltration of the police. But, in Manhattan or Oakland, the main stream of arrests and sentences is directed at blacks and Latin Americans, ghetto minorities rapidly becoming majorities. Enforced unemployment and poverty channel their lives into a certain disorder, defined as crime by the white ruling class. The actual basic function of our police is to *keep a subject urban population under control*, to protect the white suburbs from the ghetto. Since the ghetto has not yet invaded Laurel Terrace, the threat exists at present only as a guilty sense that the suburb *deserves* to be threatened. The size of the police force, both relative and absolute, is in proportion to the injustice and guilt. The more police a city swears in, the closer it stands to revolution.

America has sworn herself in as global policeman, and daily the phrase proves more apt. On every level, the police force is composed of ethnic minorities one grade higher than the population controlled: Irish cops in the black ghetto, black GI's in Asian villages. Brutality grows by reciprocal feedback: if riot control grenades are good enough for our own people, they're good enough for the gooks. The presence of the occupying forces with their riot guns, armored vehicles, incapacitating agents, dogs, helicopters, search-and-destroy missions, isn't a signal for pacification, but a signal that resentment is high enough to give the militant real support. The theory of police power is having force and to spare, doled out in measured increments to disorder or rebellion. But in

Viet Nam we see the birth of a colonial consciousness and its simultaneous refutation—instant empire.

(b) Police power as mirror of exploitation at home

A California billboard reads, "Support your local police." Back home where the police are hired by the town meeting, we felt they should support *us*. When we see legislators, some known to us as individuals, hard at work in state capitols defining new crimes, authorizing new enforcement agencies, we have the illusion that somebody somewhere is giving a mandate for change. But two iron principles can't be touched:

Whatever the ruling class needs to do must be legal. Divorce, stock-speculation, exploitation of natural products overseas, drinking at cocktail parties, gambling at resorts, real-estate deals, professional privilege of doctors and lawyers and clergy, building fortunes, safety of home jewelry, sending kids to private schools— the privilege of buying these rights must be carefully guaranteed. It's very serious to break the united front by embezzlement, manipulating the market, infringing suburban zoning regulations, talking to reporters. Even more embarrassing is to be caught in a specifically lower-class offense like smoking grass. Still, if possible, things are covered up, the offender is reeducated and brought back in; at worst he can buy lawyers and mitigating circumstances.

Any shortcuts for an oppressed class to bypass the officially designated hard road up must be illegal. Threats to property, values, law and order, routine, are put down with whatever force is necessary. Likewise whatever the authorities decree might lead to such a threat: drinking on the street, gambling in back alleys, cheap weapons, shoplifting, nonpayment of rent, drugs, treating a policeman or judge as an equal, deceiving a social worker, beating a wife, borrowing cars. The trickle of converts who make it to the top by upper-class rules can be accepted.

A society gets the police it deserves. If it hasn't got a deeply oppressed class—England before black immigration—it can operate with a minimal police force. They told us in school the police stood above class interests. But you can't obscure the fact of a ruling class which sits on the bench, makes the laws, and hires the police.

The county jail and the county mental hospital aren't all that different as one drives by. They illustrate the same mentality: out of sight, out of mind. The only long-run program to reduce brutality is deciding to get along without them, inventing flexible decentralized ways to deal with alleged incompetents and alleged criminals. Much of the clientele would evaporate as actual exploitation was reduced.

(c) Colonialism as police power

The massive oppressed populations of Africa and Asia are by-products of opening local cultures to world trade. In Latin America they're the result of intermarriage with the colonists. In the United States, a slave community was the open-eyed decision of a ruling class. It would be one step ahead to humanize the systems of exploitation already with us. But although exploration is at an end, social change can beget a new proletariat. In the three years since I have come to California I've seen a new community and style of life emerge in the hippies, with roots in the bohemians of the forties and the beatniks of the fifties, but more intense and clearly marked. If the mutation turns out to be persistent, it'll be persecuted by the Man even more than now. For present or future subject populations, the only acceptable goal is dropping out from colonial society into autonomous status.

There's certainly need for an impartial police power to regulate conflicts between roughly equal forces—Turkish and Greek Cypriotes, Israelis and Arabs, Indians and Pakistanis. (But where the United Nations fails, the United States is the last place to look for impartiality—or the secret of civil tranquility.)

The anarchy resulting from insufficient police power isn't an inner fault but a colonial heritage. The Belgians subverted tribalism in the Congo by using it as a slave-preserve; they kept local leaders from rising above elementary-school level; they sold off the mineral resources; and then as if to prove how indispensable they were, they pulled out. The organs of society were destroyed and prevented from regenerating. A single-minded ruling class can create conditions to justify its trusteeship after the fact.

We point correctly to Switzerland, Denmark, Sweden as states with minimum police power. None has an oppressed minority, all are products of the same political tradition—whose fragility is clearer than it was. We might have added the Netherlands or Belgium, until we remember how they acted in Indonesia, the Congo, South Africa. All Europe is capable of the same things; behind every quaint Guildhall façade lies a permanent possibility of the same naked coercion.

A Great Power has now so much hardware that a small nation can only challenge it in a plainly just cause. Then world opinion will keep violence below some fixed level (however high), and the liberation army can live off the country. We'll hardly see a small outlaw state again; open aggression against a Great Power is too easily put down. The Japanese in World War II gave us a good run for our money, but the outcome was never seriously in doubt; and they wouldn't have attacked us at all if we'd had atomic bombs at the beginning. Their initial attack forfeited neutral support—even though with surgical exactness against a military base, and in the end *we* mounted terrorist raids against civilian populations. A secret attack on a Great Power by a paranoid small state with a few atomic bombs could do a lot of damage, but would be suicidal.

Will the United States someday go around the world putting down oligarchic racist regimes in the name of justice? Who could trust her wielding a power so wildly out of character? Her interventions will use only the current pretext: the little guy is a stooge for another Great Power. But little guys aren't content any longer to be stooges; the virus of self-determination has gotten loose. The Establishment line of a Communist conspiracy subverts even the goals it was meant to serve.

Somebody in Washington must realize we're a principal factor pushing the Socialist world together. Why do we go on threatening then? Because we feel threatened. Not by the balance of nuclear terror, but because only socialism offers an end to corruption and land-monopoly. If Russia or China has a minority as submerged or alienated as ours, the secret is well kept. Before the Soviet invasion of Czechoslovakia in 1968 they had no troops or bases outside their own territory. It's we who combine the data into a theory of aggression; we can't imagine any motivation other than our own. The paranoid creates an actual persecution of himself; the principal force working for a Communist conspiracy is our conviction of its existence.

The problem is not whether police power should be eliminated, but whether it can be brought within tolerable limits. We were never meant to take the request about supporting local police seriously; the functional meaning of the motto is *white supremacy*—a plea to close ranks against the restless native population. Police power will be respected precisely where it becomes humanized—and unnecessary. Our job is to find some way actually in our power of destroying the roles of master and slave.

(d) The demonic state as problematical entity

Neither medicine nor history should reduce itself to pathology. Of course the effects of malfunctioning in the liver or thyroid point roughly to the purpose of normal functioning—which is harder to identify or describe in societies, since all are in part diseased. But we must believe that our description of society works best when people are finding fulfillment through life in community. Let us go on taking the New Testament seriously where many interpreters desert it. The form of society that it sees as transparent and worth analysis is the ongoing community of love. If we've begun to trust it, as a working principle we should be clearest where it's clearest, and regard as problematical the areas where it's silent or ambiguous. And for the New Testament, the basic problematical area is the State and its police power, symbolized by the demonic forces that don't bear looking into too closely.

We're told, perhaps with irony, that Caesar has a realm where certain things belong to him. If we don't pay the tax (itself an ambiguous item) he'll come and get it anyway. There's another realm, not ambiguous, that he hasn't got any access to; and it's taken for granted he'll keep asking for things from it that don't belong to him. We'll always have to deal with him in his own area; but in that other realm he's already deposed. The New Testament consistently maintains this ambiguity of feeling about the State.

Roman soldiers were in Palestine by right of conquest, which made them the only police there. The Roman Empire, unlike mod-

G

ern states, had no rival of the same kind; it looked as the United Nations would if it swallowed up most national sovereignties and made absolute claims for itself. Palestine saw that caravans in and out of Damascus were no longer attacked by Arab raiders from the desert—"broken up [Strabo says] through the law and order due to the Romans, and the security maintained by the soldiers quartered in Syria." But nobody asked the Palestinians for their preference, and it's not proved that Rome kept better order than the early Seleucids or Maccabees.

When Jesus welcomes a centurion beside a Samaritan or tax collector as an outsider capable of goodwill, it's less tolerance than treasonable collaboration. (No wonder John Baptist, conversely, fell afoul of the puppet government; imagine Venerable Tri Quang admonishing Green Berets "not to rob anybody by violence or denunciation, and to be content with their wages.") Marxists have correctly understood, and from their viewpoint correctly complained, that Jesus counsels cooperation with this arbitrary, unjust, and illegal power. As part of our program of winning over the enemy, he says we should cooperate with the draft—remembering that it only involved forced labor and not training in killing, for Caesar was more careful than Johnson about putting weapons in the hands of oppressed populations.

Paul and other writers of Epistles tell their hearers to accept the criminal law, pay taxes, pray for the Emperor as guarantor of peace—Zealot resistance, however futile, was still a live option. So was a slave revolt, and slaves are supposed to be patient when unjustly beaten, like Jesus. The master is the local embodiment of Caesar. We want at least to hear slavery condemned as wrong; but the New Testament assumes we've read the Law and the Prophets and know that already. The new way could only have arisen in an environment where armed revolt, however just, wasn't going to succeed. Our problem is to reaffirm that way where armed revolt not only deserves to succeed but very likely will—in the hills of Guatemala, Mozambique, Laos, in the flats of Newark.

We're rightly offended by two-bit dictators, a Duvalier or Salazar, who don't care if the world knows what they're like. Much more should we reject trillion-dollar exploiters who hide their reality behind a lie. The Stalin purge and the Hitler terror taught us once again that evil is real. We learned the lesson in large part through Reinhold Niebuhr, who wanted to localize it and believe America still somehow exempt. And so we explained away our treatment of the red man as a temporary fanaticism, our treatment of the Negro by economics, Hiroshima by pressure of war, degradation of the environment by ignorance, exploitation of Latin America by—I don't know what. How, we said, could a nation have fallen prey to demonic powers where citizens retained freedom to stand up and say so? How indeed? Rhetoric about "imperialism" and other old-fashioned words falls way short of a derailment so radically new in history we can't find any name for it.

The early Church explained the opposition to herself by saying that individuals have been taken over by small demonic powers, and institutions by big ones. Those beings aren't simply politicians, but they operate through politicians. When God "triumphs" over the Principalities and Powers (Aesopic language for Proconsuls and Emperors), he's giving them a taste of their own Imperial medicine.

The scene of demonic power is human society in those numerous places where it's broken down. Jesus and the Apostles weren't superstitious; they did not see malevolence working through nature or through neutral structures. "Satan" and "Beelzebul" are names for warped institutions. The interlocking of the authorities—Roman and Jewish, religious and secular, human and trans-human—isn't analyzed, just presupposed. The New Testament sees a Syndicate arrayed against us. The State is the last place to look for either our understanding of community or our program of positive renewal.

(e) True police power as environmental regulation

The normal mode of justice is for separate communities to govern their own affairs, and negotiate like Greek city-states through ambassadors. Traditionally dependent groups, women and high school students, have set up their own organizations within the peace movement, and incidentally lobbied for their rights. The prickliness of black militants comes from claiming to be ambassadors of a community that isn't yet recognized. Self-policing of a homogeneous community with no oppressed class doesn't present much of a problem. The real problem is to maintain resistance in a big community against doing violence to a little one. Anyway, it's not solved by relabeling aggression as police power. The legitimate realm of police power is to protect the really helpless—juvenile law, far from shielding kids without families, has indefinite power to push them around. Police power should protect us against things (by sanitation, inoculation, disaster relief); and things against us (by preservation of the environment).

Rich families can preserve wilderness tracts, herds of threatened animals; they're subject to pressure by taxation, but not by politics like managers of national parks. The richest American today can't remove much more than a Gardiners Island from circulation. All the serious problems involve a watershed, a continent, the globe. Biologists must persuade politicians, which can only happen in a climate of public opinion for conservation. The civil rights experience in turn suggests that law helps create public opinion. Somehow we must break into the ascending cycle.

When one sees virgin stands of redwood going under the chain saw, one is tempted to bribe the legislators. But unethical means are self-defeating. What we need is the animism of Mediterranean or primitive peoples, an instinctive ecology; the cedar of Lebanon exists as the sacred groves of the Maronite patriarch. It's hard to imagine cultivating that instinct when we can't keep rats or napalm off babies. Actually human populations can be regenerated a lot faster than biological communities. The whole English countryside was created quicker than it takes to grow a single redwood—much less a forest.

As soon as you put on your boots and get out in the country, police power and nonviolence and intelligence and mysticism become the same thing. How important is it to keep the Alaska grizzly alive? How big a breeding population is needed? How many hundred square miles will it occupy? How can we fit other things into its requirements? From time to time it's been an imperial despotism that saw these questions best. For three thousand years the Lebanese forest was harvested and preserved by successive naval powers that wanted it for timber—Egypt, Tyre, Assyria, Babylon, Persia, the Seleucids, Rome. It was the land-based Arabs who let it go. We should hope a really free society could do better. There will be plenty of things for a genuine police power to do after it gets over its current hang-up on squirting poison at living things.

3. The bankruptcy of world war

(a) Hiroshima made all the difference

Since every nation tries to get a big brother behind it, every fight has in it the seeds of the new thing called "war." What Head of State is 85 percent sure that this or that provocation will fail to spiral into pushing the red button? Modern war normally uses the means available: functionally specialized explosives and anti-personnel devices, chemical and biological poisons, incendiarism, manned and unmanned carriers, reactions creating blast and radioactivity. If an industrial Power out of deference to public opinion or tactical needs denies itself certain means, it feels the more licensed to cut loose with the others. Modern war is characterized, as we all know, by its impersonality; its indiscriminacy, threatening whole populations; the uprooting of communities into refugee camps; the danger of permanently damaging the environment which winner and loser alike must share. (Its impersonality and threat to the environment it shares with the other new thing called "peace.")

After Hiroshima we'd half-expected that any new war would be nuclear. When somebody devised a counter-insurgency equally odious on its scale, we congratulated him on his self-restraint. Viet Nam is our Spain, the trial market for new merchandise in the kind of war we'd expected not to fight. But in the poker game of bluff and counter-bluff now occupying the global rumpusroom, the actual cards are nuclear. Beside that threat, the world should be glad to run the risk of domination by Russia or China—or by the United States for that matter. No alleged justice or ideology could outweigh the massive violence to nature and society.

But nobody for a moment has given serious thought to cutting back on the production of old bombs or the invention of new ones. Industrial powers could never have been excluded from the "secret" let out of the bag at Hiroshima, that the thing could be done with brains and money. And every month since 1945 all sides have been analyzing World War III by a theory originally developed for games and economic behavior. Its paradoxes are all the policy we've got. For a nation to provide adequate shelters is reckoned the most aggressive possible act. Everything stands on making the deterrent force invulnerable against a preemptive strike. Parallel to the Distant Early Warning line, the cruising Polaris subs and the airborne alert, the Minutemen in their silos, there is now envisaged a screen of anti-missile missiles. Speculative theories are elaborated about the likely psychological reaction of a 50 percent surviving population.

This non-policy is open to two objections on its own terms:

(1) *The courses of action it proposes aren't demonstrably feasible.* The planners, with billions per annum in their pocket, are still only one among the forces affecting U.S. policy; their recommendations are subject to unpredictable compromise, which may knock out the proposed bluff or threat. Presumably they'll try to work the decisions of Congress and the Joint Chiefs of Staff into their projections. But we who are standing out there in the cold have no assurance that events and theory will converge rather than continuing to move further apart. This objection, a necessary evil in a farm program, is fatal in a life-and-death program.

(2) *The planners can never know as much as the theory requires.* The other side does its best to keep pulling surprises. We, the two hundred million recipients, can't be guaranteed to act according to predictions. The planners can't stipulate for the peace movement not to rise above a certain level of militancy; it was born without their permission. Even if they run a network of hot lines between every world capital, an essential feature of the problem is that somebody may push a panic button somewhere. "All these uncertainties have been programmed into the computer." But the future, being the future, will always introduce some new factor not taken account of in all their analyses.

We know that Hermann Kahn and his colleagues have taken maximum precautions to continue along their present line. This may prove their big miscalculation, blocking them from a change of options which their own principles should require. Thus, out of the desperation which they themselves have helped induce, revolt among a submerged population here, in sympathy with our victims overseas, is destroying precisely the America which the planners set out to defend.

(b) World War II as seed of our dilemma

The situation ushered in by nuclear energy is novel and unexampled. Our best guides are the various past situations when a radical novelty came into history. World War II might seem the least helpful parallel of all: it was the end of the old order, we're the beginning of the new. But it lay on the route which led to our present position. In the thirties and forties we were told by the realists, Christian and secular, that the only moral course was to resist Hitler with military power. Not as person but what he stood for. If you must have a personalized enemy, it can only be the demonic power. Did our military power in fact effectively resist it? Our military resistance to Hitler didn't so much prevent genocide as bring it on, since extermination camps were a product of the war. He gave advance notice as he talked himself into them; if our real intention was to save the European Jews, we took the course least well adapted to do so. At neither time when we could have taken them in as quota-free immigrants—before and after the war—did we show any interest. Rather we forced them to the Middle East, where their resettlement created exactly as many new refugees.

We not only pushed Hitler into genocide, we pushed ourselves into genocide. We adopted on the same scale, and as a permanent policy, the treatment of civilian populations which he invented. We rushed into Hiroshima mainly to avoid being indebted for Soviet assistance in the Pacific. Communiqués from Washington contain the same misrepresentations about deeds, the same rhetoric about excellence of motives, which we fought the war to end. By fighting the demon with his own weapons, you can demolish the structure he's temporarily living in—at the expense of transferring him to your own address. The demon himself is immortal. Who could imagine a clearer illustration that you become what you fight?

One is put to shame by the insight of men like Al Hassler and

Dave Dellinger, who in World War II, not knowing that nuclear
energy was in the works, still affirmed that nothing constructive
could come out of armed conflict, and went to jail rather than
cooperate with the Selective Service System. Of course, so far as
pacifism in the thirties thought it could get political agreement on
appeasement or convert the enemy to love, it was unrealistic; it
hadn't reckoned which things were in its power. So far as it retained
the benefits of upper-class status or imperialism, seeing no connection with the labor movement or the new nationalism or Negro
dignity, it was inconsistent; it hadn't worked out its position
through to the end.

World War II was the war in which at the time it was hardest
to see the true path. Looking back to the early twenties, we know
that the victors could have begun a program of reconciliation with
Germany to prevent precisely what happened. They didn't. Looking back to the late thirties, we see that demonism in Germany had
then gone beyond healing, and that elemental nationalism in England was bound to resist her. Going to jail was the most constructive course; but few of us had the power of technological prediction,
or faith in God, to see this.

Viet Nam is the war in which at the time it's easiest to see the
true path. It's a gift of Providence to Christianity and nonviolence.
So far Vietnamese nationalists haven't been dehumanized, because
they understand their own strength. Still our technology has forced
them into a severity of reprisal which will make it hard to swing
the whole nation behind them. This is the tragedy we must try to
expiate.

World War III is being prepared for all around us. When it
comes, the true way to follow will be clearer than in World War
II, less clear than in Viet Nam. *Now* is the time to be maximizing
possibilities of reconciliation. As it comes closer, our range of action will become more and more restricted. But we already know
the true way. The needs of the biological environment, simple
survival of peasant communities around the world, are the polestar
which always orients us. Men of goodwill know this; the urgency
is to guide their sentiment into action.

(c) A more excellent way

The little band of resisters in World War II were led by intuition to see that the course of action was "right" which history now vindicates as expedient. If I judge that any serious war may well bring in the nuclear capacity of the Great Powers, from this pragmatic judgment I reach the conclusion—as absolute as any conclusion can be—that large-scale war won't do any more.

We've got to go beyond the balance of fear, and fear is overcome only by confidence. After our best political analysis, we've got to affirm that people will only move towards confidence by starting to trust each other, before the full evidence for their reliability has been processed in the computers. What's most needed is groups known to be consistently working for international goodwill, agencies like the American Friends Service Committee, which can be slandered neither by a Pentagon nor by the most fanatical insurgent. Any such group should meet the following conditions:

(1) Its commitment to social welfare and nonviolent reconciliation is so clearly defined, and deeply ingrained, that no illiterate anywhere can suspect it of other motives.

(2) It has an attractive ideology, so that people who see it in action are induced to do the same thing out of the same motives.

(3) It has so stable a family and institutional base, that it will obviously still be operating from the same principles ten years, a generation, a hundred years, from now.

(4) It spreads its presence out fairly, so that no one part of the world gets ahead of another.

Since nobody can invent social movements out of whole cloth, this is the description of an international religion—not quite fulfilled by any one currently operative. It's a Buddhism less ascetic than now and more concerned in theory with social justice. It's a Quakerism which has recovered Fox's passionate sense of mission, bringing the poor to share its motivation and vision. It's a Communism converted to nonviolence, a Castroism become altruistic. It's a Christian mission cut away from its paralyzing Establishment in Western colonial powers and the just-war theory.

Whatever international confidence we now enjoy rests on individuals and groups which begin to meet these conditions. The ideal already exists in the hearts of learned and simple around the world; one who has taken this burden on himself is recognized even when he doesn't carry any placard. Anybody who's begun to find himself in the role of such an ambassador will testify that its most transforming tendency is on himself.

The thing is to take the present alignment of forces as simply given, and then subtract from it uniformly all the way around. Imagine thousands of American hostages spread out in the villages of North Viet Nam, Cuba, Bolivia, Guatemala; thousands of Russian students spending a year of study in the States. Since we can't count on influencing the arms race, or national politics, or the police power which upholds both, our cue is to de-emphasize and desanctify them, making other forms of endeavor more exciting, leaving them to wither on the vine. An all-out effort is indicated to divert men and money from destructive jobs to constructive ones. The cutting edge which proves our seriousness to others and ourselves is resolute non-cooperation with military conscription.

A realistic middle-term hope would be to help catalyze a Russian peace movement—not so urgent as ours currently, but in the end indispensable. The preconditions are there in the broad spectrum of Orthodox spirituality, the pacifist novel, the liberalization of Soviet society. We would need an international cadre fluent in Russian; committed to the peace and freedom movement in the United States, Latin America, and Asia; and well-versed in Marxism. A Russian peace movement, no doubt after many setbacks, would give our peoples a real link on terms of equality; our leaders would have a common cause for complaint, for détente. Useful communication on a new level would have begun.

Any institution, however informal, which begins to meet these conditions is of course also liable to Establishment. Not even Quakers can count on breeding true to type. We must pin our hopes on a dynamic shifting reform movement (its exact place only visible to a contemporary by moral insight) at the heart of a society paying lip service to justice. Those better acquainted with Buddhism must make any adjustments necessary in my description. For Westerners, I hope I've shown that this current need is precisely what Jesus intended to meet. But if Christianity is to serve any such function, it must come to terms with its symbolism. The New Testament validates its nonviolence above all through a myth of the end of the world. We must come to terms with this myth through our own situation.

4. The myth of the end of the world

(a) New Testament ethics and eschatology

Once violence has begun, it's hard to stop short of maximum capability. But we daren't use it because we're capable of too much; our inventiveness has priced violence out of the planetary market. We don't know what necessary feature will go first under heavy enough assault by war &' pollution: the will to survive and reproduce; the structure of a manageable society; an undamaged genetic pool; or some maximum tolerable radiation level in the environment. When we imagine the pathology of breakdown, as society is reduced to an ever more primitive level, the inseparability of culture from environment becomes clearer. The culture of southeastern Asia *is* the rice paddies of the delta; destruction of the fields is both physical and spiritual genocide. We're reduced to hoping simply that there will be time for shame and world opinion to overthrow the violent one before the final whistle.

We found the bankruptcy of violence affirmed in the New Testament long ago—but not apparently for quite these reasons. It sees both the nonviolence of the poor, and the exploitation practiced by the powerful, as necessarily their own reward. The announcement of that necessity alters the previous state of affairs, for it polarizes society; the son of man comes to bring division. The scene of this division is a time of troubles, which is symbolized as a double change of the whole environment. The physical order breaks down because of the sins of the violent; but also in some realm the earth is restored for the inheritance of the poor. The breakdown appears as a new flood, a universal conflagration: "As it was in the days of Noah . . . as it was in the days of Lot . . . so will it be on the day when the son of man is revealed."

The Hebrew, who sees a transcendent agency as having once

organized a universe out of tidal chaos, faces up to the possibility
that justice may bring everything back to original status: "I looked
on the earth, and lo, it was waste and void." Late Judaism elaborated this apocalyptic theme for its own sake, apart from the historical and ethical concerns which originally motivated it. With Jesus,
the arrival of the last days, "eschatology," becomes the central
symbolism for a radical intensification of moral concern. Different
reports of his teaching, as well as its echoes in other books, are
unequal in the accuracy with which they grasp the novelty; but the
spectrum of variations points to an incandescent source.

If we've dated Paul's letters in the right order, he comes more
and more to see the Last Things as daily occurrence in the community of love: "If ye then be risen with Christ, seek those things
which are above" (Col. 3:12); "the night is far spent, the day is at
hand" (Rom. 13:12). This was a necessary reaction against the
literal symbolism in the young Paul (the Thessalonian correspond-
ence), and in the unsatisfactory discourse that Mark attributes to
Jesus at the Temple. But something essential is lost in Paul's "realized eschatology." The effect of Jesus' symbolism is to place before
us the destruction of the whole environment, natural and social,
not as an hypothesis, but as a possible deserved event; and then
have us reconsider who and what we are. Eschatology is necessary
to his ethics.

(b) The problem of New Testament eschatology

One of the best post-nuclear apocalypses is Bob Dylan's "It's
a Hard Rain's A-Gonna Fall." "Hard rain" combines fallout and
flood, destruction by fire and water. It works as a timeless lament
over the fall of an exploitative society; it's made more pointed when
we learn that it was generated by the Cuban missile crisis. Dylan's
symbols have maximum availability. Jesus couldn't have been a
worse poet than Dylan. But the fossilization of his poetry into
dogma has raised Cyclopean walls against recovering its original
freshness. Theological scholastics vacillate between the poles of a
dilemma:

(1) Jesus and his earlier followers were under the misappre-

hension that the world would literally end in their generation; later New Testament writings struggle to escape from what they see to be an error.

(2) Jesus uses this symbolism as the most forcible way to speak about timeless truths; Paul misunderstood him at first, but in later letters returns to the original meaning.

Both sides of the dilemma do injustice to poetry. The myth of the end of the world marks an intrinsic connection between our natural environment and the social environment where individual sin and redemption happen. It also looks ahead to the end of this or that world-empire, and to the birth of a servant society within its fall. Its force rests on the fact that it points to something real coming. The myth of the end of the world points to the fact of the end of the world. That future truly casts its shadow before it; the exhaustion of fresh water in this spring or lake is an early phase of ultimate environmental breakdown, however many million years away.

The Bible sees the earth as the planned environment of man, whose job is to till and keep it. In the covenant with Noah, God almost promises an indefinite continuance of the earth. In that case it might seem sufficient recompense for our death if we were continued without end through the seed of our loins. In a society where a man's individuality is defined through his family, this is a real immortality. But if the earth won't continue indefinitely, another kind of recompense must be found. The myth of the end of the world is a difficulty for the Jew; why did he invent it?

(c) Technology as the fulfillment of eschatology

The biblical writers saw that man was given radical power and responsibility. By individual decisions he could maintain or corrupt himself as a center of organization. By collective decisions individually ratified, he could maintain or corrupt his society as a center of organization. In the continuity which the Bible sees between nature and history, it also has to say, "By the collective decision of humanity, ratified by individuals, it can maintain or corrupt the created order as a center of organization." It saw man as so organic in nature, and sin as so deep-rooted in man, that it correctly guessed nature couldn't remain permanently immune to the effects of sin.

The prophet in his historical analysis says that catastrophe happens because a principle labeled as the noun Yahweh makes it happen, in recompense for individual and corporate sin. Faced with the sins of an individual nation, God hasn't got any recourse but to raise up an Assyrian against its citadel—while perhaps reserving the human seedcorn of the future. Faced with the sins of the human race, God hasn't got any recourse but to raise up his power, previously creative, and destroy the environment.

When the Hebrew says that something will be done by God as ultimate cause, he doesn't exclude the possibility that it'll happen through an historical human agency; on the contrary, he normally implies it. When the prophet envisages God destroying the nation, he sees Assyria as the rod of his anger. Amos lists among intolerable things atrocities in warfare (violation of sepulture, killing pregnant women) and entrenched class injustice at home (selling the poor into debt-slavery). With our Greek mode of historical analysis we see that these things set one little Syrian state against another, class against class, so that Assyria could pick them off one at a time. Evidently then the prophet, who gives us all our data, saw it too in his Hebrew mode of historical analysis. He also found it important to name the principle by which injustice brings self-destruction, and make that noun the subject of verbs. We easily believe that Jesus saw the coming destruction of the Temple, and could have told us it would be Roman hands that were laid on the stones.

Each ancient generation ran the physical environment downhill, but so insensibly that few noticed it. At first, calamities of the environment are projected into the past; the stories of Noah and Lot received final form a little before Amos. The prophet has the primordial Sea rising up like the Nile and once again destroying the works of man. As the canon of legend was closed, destruction of the environment could only be projected onto the future as a myth of the end of the world—where cosmic justice and proto-science also demanded it.

The biblical writers didn't know how the planet's fabric could be destroyed by human agency. But if such a means should appear, it would fit Hebrew modes of speaking to say that God used a human agency to vindicate his justice. The appearance of technology in our own days resolves the problem created by the myth of the end of the world. It finally roots eschatology back in its soil of prophecy. In fact, technology isn't merely a vindication but a result of prophetism; it's one more manifestation of the freedom which prophecy both recorded and created.

The Hebrew Bible operates on a level where science, history, and existential concern haven't yet been crystallized into independent disciplines. The first chapters of Genesis are at once a speculative version of planetary origins, a reconstruction of the stages in human society, and a symbolic account of the birth of freedom and sin in Everyman. (Hesiod does the same things, not so well.) Today we've come to see that in this unrolling universe, science and history and religion are partly arbitrary slices at different angles across the roastbeef of reality. The independent discipline of each has become so powerful that it's easy to overlook their essential areas of overlap. Therefore those early unitary myths are a permanent necessity of our continuing education.

(d) The final dimension of prophecy

The political prophet, besides pointing out the realities of the present, genuinely grasps the inevitable near future when he sees as already operative the forces which will necessarily produce it. If I see a bomb falling from a plane I know that a particular sequence will follow. He also grasps the distant future to the extent that it repeats features of the present. The myth of the end of the world is a true anticipation of technology. Through it the eschatological prophet genuinely grasps, not the repetitive, but the novel features of the distant future.

The Old Testament myth of creation is a true proto-science: its interest in the ocean, clay, sexuality, consciousness, is a correct insight into the essential features of past evolution. The New Testament myth of the end of the world is a true foreshadowing of demonic technology; it sees the destruction of the physical environment as a direct consequence of social violence. In the Apocalypse of John, the rivers and fountains of water become blood when the angel pours in the bowl of God's anger—because men shed the blood of saints and prophets. As the creation-myth pierces back to the beginning, the prophetic myth pierces through to the end; together (in contrast to Greek cyclic theories) they block out the evolutionary parabola of the planet.

The End also vindicates the blessedness of those now exploited, at a Messianic banquet whose scene is a new earth under a new sky. Adam was supposed to keep the garden of the earth, using his police power for ecological management; Paul identifies him as Christ, pattern of restored humanity. Destruction and fulfillment of the environment are held together in tension. Although it's said to be God who does all this, the style of biblical thought requires man to be his agent. Jesus validates ethics by eschatology; ours is the first generation where the truth of his words has emerged from faith into history.

We saw that our new powers had rendered world war obsolete. Jesus said that violence belonged to the old Age. We thought he meant this in some mystical sense; the self-destruction of violence took place in the soul of the possessor. But his images state that what once was whispered behind closed doors will be proclaimed from rooftops; the secret murder in a man's heart will be spread across burning continents. What we thought our expedient nuclear pacifism is identical with the expedient pacifism of Jesus, which announces woes on the self-deceiving violent. Prophecy gives up its secrets in these last times.

We tell ourselves that not every war leads to world war. But the Bible states that the remotest possible consequences of everything will really happen. A principle of radical accuracy is built into history. If every war leads in principle to world war, only nonviolence will do.

5. Violence in a people's revolution

(a) The just-war theory revisited

Establishment Churches can't be pacifist, or they'd destroy that usefulness to the State which defines them. Therefore, to keep up a decent token respect for the Gospel, they must hold in theory that some wars are just and some aren't. This necessity is a hot potato. Without protest until recently, they let the American State pass conscientious-objection laws which recognized only objectors to *all* war. In fact, that was the only kind of objector the Churches produced until Viet Nam; the young men got their views from Quakers or similar groups and ignored the official position of their own Churches, much to the relief of Church and State. This clandestine recognition of pacifism canonized a double-standard morality: Gospel precepts were relegated to a few idealists, while the bulk of Christians made the world's necessary compromises.

When the Viet Nam draft resisters moved from absolutism to the just-war theory, the Churches had to face up to the demands of justice. Traditional pacifism, which needn't make any application of morality to politics, often reduces to what I call Establishment nonviolence. The necessary first step from it was selective conscientious objection, which makes a judgment on a particular war. The just-war theory is a transitional ally of the Law and the Prophets, which speaks the message of justice to the Establishment. But we must go one stage beyond that theory (three stages beyond the Establishment Churches) to the Gospel, which speaks the message of nonviolence to the Revolution. We must make an unremitting application of morality to *all* political situations, present and future.

The Churches recognize in practice what their theologians missed in theory: the traditional marks of the just war reduce to a single criterion; *a just war is one fought by my side.* It might seem then as if the Churches relegated the possibility of unjust wars to theory only. Not at all, there are just as many of them; *an unjust war is one fought by the other side.* I know a Catholic who holds the just-war theory, but maintains there isn't any point of view from which the Viet Nam war could be considered just. Did he consider the point of view of the Vietnamese? Could he justify not having become a Viet Cong partisan? The actual process of moral reflection isn't directed at the details of an existing war, but at choosing the right side.

A revolutionary is a patriot who changed sides when he discovered where justice lay. An Establishment is a partial revolution

H

which has succeeded and forgotten its origins. The Establishment patriot and the revolutionary agree in *having a side*. The just-war theory reduces to the same truism for each. With a difference, although both give their conduct the benefit of the same doubts, the cause of the revolutionary happens to be objectively just. But as soon as he begins to think out of partisanship rather than objectivity, his logic is assimilated to the patriot's.

How could a war fought by my side fail to be just? It's declared by a *legitimate authority*: namely, the one that after careful thought I stayed with. It's being fought for a *just cause*: namely, the policy I've always supported, that I've helped form. In *self-defense*: I know my side doesn't have any imperial ambitions; it wants only security for its legitimate interests, small or great; it certainly doesn't want to police the faceless enemy on his own soil. As a *last resort*: I don't want to get shot at; I instructed my government to try first every way short of war. With *moderate means*: I know our own humanitarian motives, and I respect world opinion; so I instruct my generals to avoid unnecessary civilian casualties, to use the minimum force necessary, to work toward the quickest solution. With means *proportionate* to the goals: we who're doing the fighting are hardheaded about manpower and resources; we won't throw good money after bad. For *limited goals*: we've got better things to do than go out and conquer the world. With *reasonable hope of success*: even in a case of ultimate self-defense or grave danger, I know that my generals won't go into action without some plan, however desperate.

This universal logic of the just-war theory takes a special form in each generation. It was self-evident to Augustine that the decaying Empire and newly established Church deserved to be fought for against pagan barbarians; to the Crusaders that the Holy Places deserved defense against Islam; to the counter-Reformation that the wars of the Conquistadores would bring the greatest of benefits —baptism for the heathen; to Soviet revolutionaries that maintaining secure frontiers was a happy prerequisite for future world Communism. The reader may fill in the wars he knows best. Prof. Ramsey, who discusses how nuclear war may be made just, illustrates the flexibility of Christian doctrine for contemporary relevance.

The criteria of the just war don't emerge from the Gospel by any process of subtraction or accommodation; rather from the two facts that I have a side, and that I esteem myself a person of normal consistency. If I, being the reasonable man that I am, can continue living on this side, I know in advance that whatever it does will agree with my principles. The Gospel asks us to reject both facts. We learn from it what our hearts confirm: we're full of inconsistency. We also learn that the justice of even the right side is relative; finally our only side can be humanity.

Certainly at Gethsemane all criteria of the just war were met. Several times Jesus had been proclaimed a legitimate leader. He had the justest of causes: to teach the new way of reconciliation to followers who still missed the point. The situation was self-defense (and defense of his friends) against an illegal mob, as a last resort when months or years of teaching and going underground had failed. He had the limited goal of getting back home and starting again, with good prospect of success; the moderate means of a quick scuffle in the dark in which no adversary might even be seriously wounded. But as soon as blood is shed, he gives up all resistance.

I'd always assumed this was the Gospel itself, defined by the Sermon on the Mount and illustrated by the Cross. "If my kingdom were of this world, my servants would fight" (John 18:30). Reinhold Niebuhr agrees with this view of what Jesus was, and clearly states that it's a delusion to think we can use him as a model for society. Then why have so many people thought it important to call themselves his followers? Perhaps we feel the need for some doctrine to tell us that what we're doing is wrong. Islam, which explicitly states the doctrine we all follow—that our side is superior and deserves to be propagated by the sword—hasn't had anything like the same success; we can't forgive the Prophet for having let the cat out of the bag.

(b) Solidarity with a people's revolution

Around the Third World, a venal oligarchy of landowners and military is the local agent of colonialism, political or economic. Almost any liberation movement, whatever its excesses of cruelty or dogmatism, has the balance of justice on its side. The solid core of truth in Marxism lines Russia up with the liberation movements; our need for guaranteed overseas markets lines us up against them. If they weren't Socialist in the beginning, the logic of their situation pushes them into it. If a local liberation movement doesn't exist, it should. *The only serious candidate for a just war today is the people's war of liberation.*

When we read in the papers about some new guerrilla movement or program of land-reform, it's already too late. The worldwide Church has been in Latin America for hundreds of years, consistently on the side of injustice. Our fathers could have said something and didn't. The language of every oppressed people in the world is studied in our universities; U.S. corporations have big investments in them. Those knowledgeable persons, whom I've let speak for me by default, have only by exception considered the real interests of the target areas. The locals gave justice-loving people elsewhere plenty of opportunity to stop doing nothing before they took matters into their own hands.

How far should we affirm our solidarity with a violent cause? We must first be clear what isn't violence. In any case it'll be necessary to expropriate industries and assets, to redistribute land. The current owners won't volunteer; coercion must be exercised by law or arms. The revolutionaries must come to power by the ballot or military *coup d'état.* Before then they'll need a political organization, legal or illegal. Nothing so far necessarily implies violence against persons.

If the *coup d'état* involves executing fifty officers, as world history goes this is a small piece of violence, without apologizing for it, we may be thankful for having gotten off so cheap. The revolutions of Nasser in Egypt, of Castro in Cuba, in their different degrees of completeness were less painful than the country had a right to expect. And the less the liberation forces allow themselves to be co-opted by a military junta, the more guerrilla warfare and reprisals we're likely to see. If Big Brother comes in to protect freedom, every liberation movement can become a Viet Nam.

We know the landlords will resist, perhaps to the death. They aren't interested in surviving the system of privilege which has defined their class. Unless the revolution has some radical religious ideology behind it, it must be prepared to use violence; otherwise it doesn't mean business. But if it doesn't mean business it'll be co-opted by the ruling class as soon as it appears—or rather, it'll always have been their stooge. Then, unless a local religious tradi- tion of nonviolence has been radicalized into social concern, *a necessary condition for a just revolutionary movement is its willing- ness to use violence.*

(c) The role of the American overseas

Identification isn't a question of abstract advocacy, but of what we can properly and effectively do. If both sides are currently engaging in some form of violence, no position is completely pure —least of all detachment, which means passively supporting the status quo. Our initial act must be to dissociate ourselves from active injustice (which presumably accounts for some of our afflu- ence) and go over to our natural allies.

But finding the right side still doesn't take us very far. If this really is one world, and we've been benefiting at the expense of other parts, each of us has a duty to get out of America for a while and find out what's going on over there. To get in touch with one revolutionary is to get in touch with all. But few people in America are working to create conditions for honest residence overseas— many more are advertising counter-insurgency helicopters for Latin American governments.

We'll do harm rather than good, most of all to ourselves, if we get on the plane owing advance loyalty to the State Department, or to a corporation which is extracting oil, tin, bananas. One will live in a Little America overseas whose attitudes are reinforced by the only foreigners one meets—collaborationists who tell us what we want to hear. Missionaries have a dual commitment: to the exiled American military, embassy, business community; and to the privileged pro-American group of early converts, now often busi- nessmen also. American educational enterprises overseas are heavily financed by the State Department; foreign students are channeled through scholarship aid into such specialties (like teach- ing elementary English) as *we* deem appropriate.

Once the American has found some halfway credible format

for his residence, he must keep enough in the good graces of Washington and the local regime to stay on. The two years of Peace Corps is enough time to acquire some immunity to dysentery and pick up some language. A man's successor won't build on his foundations, since society is a network of personal contacts. If you stay on though, one day you'll be invited to a wedding or funeral at the house of your student or associate. He may come to trust you enough to get angry at your income. You may discover what political party he really belongs to. Actual conversation has begun. The tables are now turned; our credibility overseas rests on our political record at home.

As we put down roots, we need to find a local form of ideology for our concerns. Christianity on the scene may be fossilized and corrupt or new and eccentric or missionary-dominated. In any case we can try and interpret it to the local revolutionaries and vice versa. If we're in a Buddhist land we can start to do what the Churches should have done long before—enter into dialogue with it.

Do we go overseas expecting to receive more than we give? For at least we'll discover what it's like to live in a country that's not top dog. At the same time we're not to fall into the arrogance of certainty that Americans will provide the leadership. We slip back into wanting milkshakes, and hesitate before the investment of mastering a new language. There's an even bigger job of rebuilding back home which it's *our* duty to carry out. The real agents of reconciliation may come from some unexpected source, a small neutralist power; we'll do well to recognize them when they show up.

(d) Nonviolence in a people's revolution

We cling to the just-war theory for our side, out of a defect in self-confidence; unless we hit the enemy (we feel) we'll simply be wiped out. But looking back we may guess that our side was the winning one all along, and our militarism was the defect in our success, not its cause. The liberation movements possess the future precisely because their cause is just. This isn't our cue to let the inevitable take its course—rather to help base their victory on the best foundations. In one sense, because of their political lag, they're not our contemporaries; they can't skip stages altogether, and need their own revolution. But they're our contemporaries in the sense that they can build nuclear devices if they really want to; so their revolution must take some new shape.

It often seems as though the Church can only break loose from her Establishment ties by allying herself to the revolution without qualification, letting it be the judge of its own methods. This conclusion, which imposes itself above all on observers of the Latin American scene like Richard Shaull, does only credit to their concern for justice and for Church renewal. But the revolutionary is also capable of injustice. The more necessary the revolution, the more directly the new society will emerge from it. The time to build more justice into the new society is at the revolution. The revolutionary is indignant at the connivance of the Established Church with injustice; he knows that she's supposed to bring moral judgment into politics. If priests or doctors are willing to share their glutinous rice and the chance of napalm, they needn't compromise their witness by asking them to throw grenades also. It's an even bigger coup for them to retain their nonviolent presence than to win foreign partisans.

We must reckon with the possibility that the new peoples won't merely run their own affairs, but also get into the driver's seat. A great burst of cultural and technological energy might set a Great Power in South America, southeast Asia, Africa, India, after a few centuries. The arguments against militarism which we found applicable to us today will also work for them. The nature of the biological environment, the threats of radiation and pollution, won't have changed. If it's self-deception to say, "Revolution today, nonviolence tomorrow," then they shouldn't believe it any more than we. It's one more colonial insult to assume that they're in a pre-modern phase where violence is less dangerous than for us. To treat other people as our equals is to consider them capable of our strength and our weakness. It's uncharitable and risky to hold them up to the standard of going through the same cycle of mistakes that we did. Everything we know about history suggests that we're entering a new period which will either do better or worse than the past. Frantz Fanon feels that violence, besides being a political necessity, may be required to restore the self-respect of colonialized peoples.

But he also says:

> If we want to turn Africa into a new Europe . . . then let us leave the destiny of our countries to Europeans. They will know how to do it better than the most gifted among us. But if we want humanity to advance a step further, if we want to bring it up to a different level than that which Europe has shown us, then we must invent and we must make discoveries.

If the Buddhists in Viet Nam couldn't get up an effective nonviolent movement, much less will we. Our Establishment pacifists haven't any difficulty staying on good terms with the exploitative State and benefiting from its violence. It should involve less mental split for us to acquire identification with a just revolution, and leave the insurgents to do their thing while we do ours. They will in any case. The one creative option actually in our power is to humanize their use of force by our presence.

(e) Black Power and white support

Overseas we can be under an illusion of playing a role in the liberation. Actually we're likely to be told that our adherence, while highly valued, isn't the key factor; they'll liberate themselves by their own efforts. Our task is to remake our own society. When we do get home, we're brought up short to see how little we can do to free somebody else on this scene either.

The militancy of young black leaders in putting down their former white supporters should be an intellectual and moral relief. I used to think that the future ecclesiastical historian, looking back to twentieth-century America for a bona fide Church, would settle on black Christianity. Actually the Negro Church was too good to be true; it turns out not to have given a correct report of its members' actual feelings.

At the Chicago "Black Nation" conference of November 1967, my informant Jane Barney reports a consensus that Black Christianity

> must work to erase the mark of slavery at its deepest levels, nurture pride and self-esteem, and affirm (as does the Old

Testament) violence *for justice*—distinguishing this from all
the violence, hidden and overt, slow and sudden, legalized and
lawless, which over the centuries has worked to perpetuate
injustice and is now the oppressive force negatively shaping
the black community.

This is what black Christians *ought* to hold today, living in the
climate created by Reinhold Niebuhr where white Christians were
told to resist injustice by force. "Violence is as American as cherry
pie." We applauded the principles of the nonviolent black leaders,
praised them for seeing what had been hidden from the white
Church. But it was all wrong for a big Negro community to follow
on continuously from slavery into nonviolence, without ever having been offered revolution. Cesar Chavez, fasting as witness
against violence to his strikers, shows deeper insight into the real
alternatives.

Never again can we let ourselves get in the position of recommending nonviolence for somebody else—especially when we'd be
the ones threatened by his revolution. So long as we keep a foothold
in the bastion of that American Christianity which has become the
opiate of the middle classes, we've got no business running other
people's lives for them. Programs which siphon off the most docile
30 percent of the black community are just going to make matters
worse. We're in no position to object that we can't draw a map of
the Black Nation. Neither can the black, but he knows it's got to
come. As his situation in America is unique, the solution will have
to be also. We whites are in no position to say that the partition
of India and Pakistan is an inadmissible precedent.

It shook the white man up, as it was meant to, when the SNCC
militants talked about buying guns. The subservience of the Pull-
man porter ought to have shaken us up long before and didn't. Our
reward for failing to read resentment between the lines of servility
is the chance to read self-respect between the lines of belligerency.
He has been a master all along at reading contempt between the
lines of paternalism. Nonviolence is something we can offer to
others only so far as we illustrate it ourselves; and the nonviolent
man is the man clothed in armor who can appear on the same
platform with the advocate of violence, not be hurt by it, and keep

communications open. If his presence there is misunderstood and
he's hurt, his self-understanding in the role of reconciliation hasn't
gone very deep. When the fighting begins, we may legitimately
bring medicine, legal aid, food, or observe the police—remembering both what love demands and where justice lies.

As students of history we can help give the black man the
confidence of the Vietnamese. His fascination with shooting may
reflect a fear that his revolution isn't going to go off. We can give
him reason to believe it will—the United States someday will
become or contain a black nation, as under John Kennedy in some
sense it became an Irish nation. If the black is likely to win, it's not
too early for him to start thinking about the burdens of power and
plan to do better than we did.

If his revolution assumes a nonviolent form, it'll have to be an
indigenous one. For three hundred years we have provided the
blacks with a nonviolent ideology which we didn't have any use
for ourselves. That role is obviously finished. Our integration theory is finished too unless they choose to return to it. Now that the
old ways of solidarity between us have been shown to be unreal,
both sides must think and work creatively to find a genuine
solidarity. It exists already in the peace movement, which enjoys
an actual common concern. It's important and touching that some
black militants have married white girls.

We must say we don't want to exercise violence ourselves on
behalf of the black man; we can work in some parts of his struggle
but not in others. That doesn't mean we're deciding which his
legitimate leaders are. Only he can do that for himself, and we must
abide by his decisions—and not say we think he's making a mistake,
for the majority of his people are wherever they are, irrespective
of what we think.

As motivation we won't allow ourselves to forget that he's got
something of critical importance to teach us which we can't learn
from anybody else—in any case the thing which the master has to
learn from the slave. Already his music has given us our heart back
again. European efficiency, individualism, dynamism, have shown
us how to dominate the planet and each other. African spontaneity,

solidarity, adaptability, may be the key to living with it and with each other.

6. The scene of our actual power

(a) Summary: the obsolescence of war

Somewhere between the war that's so big as to threaten the planet, and the war that's so little as to be clearly colonialist, can't we find some war with evenly matched adversaries which will meet our standards and be pronounced just? But the cue for a third party isn't to justify a war but to reconcile it; for *we* won't find ourselves a party to the proposed just conflict. And this small equal war presumes that no Great Power will become involved. Karl Barth took as type-class of just war the self-defense of Switzerland against an invader. If that happened, we'd be as indignant as he—that is, the Great Powers would get involved. Does he wish to risk nuclear war for the sake of Switzerland? And what's the national meaning of Switzerland if not reconciliation? Only the locals know how to live off her mountains; after a time of troubles they would insensibly take over again.

What is this desire to find a just war somewhere sometime? Plenty of wars will still be fought, as the world goes, without needing our approval. Whenever we find reasons to approve some war, our own military Establishment will always be first in line to step into the slot we've made. When it's finished, we'll be faced with the same problems as before, in more intractable form—after having once again placed a moratorium on the Gospel. Barth also says that, apart from the exceptions, the whole orientation of the Churches, of humanity, should be towards peace. But so long as the exceptions are there in the textbooks, they're the only thing the Army chaplains and Secretaries of State will ever see.

It's been said that nonviolence isn't possible for us, it's a pretense to virtue greater than we've got. But what the morning paper says is that violence isn't possible for us anymore; it's escalated itself out of our league. As the fabric of life in our cities decays, the last problem we need worry about is providing for their defense against a foreign invader. Our war setup isn't maintained by any human agency at all, but by the self-perpetuating power of an institution sucking in functionaries. We've been freed from the compulsiveness of having to support something that is useless and self-perpetuating.

The State claims to know what its thing is. I say that our thing is to help raise up a class of people for whom radical reconciliation across all barriers is an individual concern, a family tradition, an institutional witness, who decide on a profession and take a job on the basis of its usefulness. What's indicated isn't a public relations campaign inventing a phony image of ourselves, but actual goodwill embodied in the travel back and forth of persons, groups, money, the arts of peace.

The problem of violence is like the problem of dirt—putting something different in its place. "If you wish peace, prepare for *peace.*" Constructive permanent communities are propagated in the same way as biological organisms: old ones making young ones. The discoveries of freedom and love are unrepeatable events, but nearly all their consequences still remain to be drawn. The ideal construction called Church History, generated by the portrait of a holy family, rests on the correct instinct that the better way is a golden thread running back to the origins of humanity. The revolution inaugurated by the Suffering Servant and Prometheus, like any other technique or language, is only learned by watching somebody else do it.

The time won't recur when good men will need to declare another closed season on reconciliation, and once again have recourse to modern war. If we were faced with invasion by intelligent non-human beings, we'd have to make a decision as to whether they were our kind. For human beings the decision has already been made; they're the ones we're never entitled to give up on. Modern war can never again be the lesser of two evils. If it breaks out anyway, and one side has a substantial claim to justice, we'll say so, and not let an identification with the unjust side stand by default. In any case we'll continue resistance to violence which supports injustice and reconciliation from wherever we are. Reconciliation is a road that never ends. It may lead to martyrdom along the way, but we've always affirmed that martyrdom isn't a dead end either, but rather the thing we're built on.

In saying that violence is hereafter ruled out, we've only taken the necessary but negative first step. Ahead lies the endless road of working it out in practice. "Nonviolence" isn't the solution of any problem; it's the discovery that no solution can be found along a certain road, which liberates us to look for one in the only area where it can be found. If we fail the first time we try again.

"But any society, including the one you make this protest in, needs minimal security; destroy it, and you destroy your own base of operations. You're a parasite on the State."—It's *not* providing security: not overseas; nor here, if all over the world people are coming to hate us. Our security lies in the goodwill that the peace movement can retain. The Government is a parasite on us.

"Should we not shackle the madman on the loose, even at the risk of hurting him?" —If we can, has he been identified?

"You propose to lay our country open to an unprincipled enemy." —Today *it* is the unprincipled enemy. We take the Government for granted, and try to create a counter-organization of society that will do the critical jobs the Government is failing at.

"Suppose little yellow men with fixed bayonets were coming at your mother or your sister." —Where in the world is this happening? This implausible scenario is guilty projection of the more familiar scene where big white men with fixed bayonets are coming at the mother and prostituting the daughter.

"Somebody must take thought for the government." —This is an illusion it tries to foster. Actually the Government takes thought for itself by an automatic momentum; this is the fact we need a counterweight for.

"If moderates don't control the Government the extremists will." —The extremists control it already. We keep trying the long shot of getting the moderates in, but we don't pin our hopes to it.

"You don't allow any place for people working inside the system for something short of perfection." —Such people always overestimate the amount of good they can do and underestimate the amount of compromise they make. Compromise will take care of itself; we don't need to worry about it. The only way to start a better way going is to start.

(b) On not being an Establishment jester

It's easy to get put inside a ball of cotton candy. The Establishment understands very well the symbolic power of morality over us—and how easily we can be gotten to settle for the name only. So it institutionalizes prophecy, provides hats of its own design for us to wear. All around us are Establishment jesters. Old ladies may carry picket signs; student papers may print editorials; the clergy may preach about peace on Christmas Eve; academicians may knock the Establishment (preferably not in their own field); overage generals may go soft in the head after retirement; Senators may talk about U.S. imperialism—provided they campaign on pork barrel projects.

It takes some time getting used to the role; a longer time to realize that one is being had. Then when we tumble to the fact that we're going through a farce, that the real decisions are being made somewhere else by guys who discounted us long ago, we've put too big an investment of time and credibility into the role. Once again criticism has been encapsulated, and the exploitation machine lumbers on. We learn to say our piece so that it can be dismissed as non-serious. We wait until we rise high enough that our criticism will be really effective—that is, never. Former Government officials would like us to believe that their resignation last year sprang from disagreement with policy. Why didn't they say so at the time? Because they were too busy negotiating their termination settlement.

The politician must have an actual constituency whose interests he serves. The nonviolent methods of Gandhi and Nehru really fitted local needs. If the United States ever gets a President with a genuine concern for world opinion, for minorities here, he'll have to be a black man—moderate enough to capture the white liberals, just radical enough that the black militants will vote for him from lack of anybody better.

The Government insists on responsible participation in the

electoral process to channel as much of our energies as possible into it. The electoral process is *its* system, which it believes it can control. But it gives the show away by operating in quite a different manner itself. The most effective Federal agencies are immune to the elective process, not subject to judicial review, exempt from criticism: the military and its Chiefs of Staff, the Federal Bureau of Investigation and its director, the Selective Service System and its director, the Central Intelligence Agency ... The President can't control these outfits; he just knows the guys on top and works with them. Government is actually conducted by a network of personal relations.

(c) The reality of Establishment power as our cue

Behind the elaborate subterfuge of role-playing stands a group of actual men—wielding power, manipulating each other by influence, blackmail, horse trading, threat, bribes, contracts, mutual interest, intermarriage, joint membership. The power behind the Establishment is people. They know each other's connections too well to be afraid that somebody will rock the boat. If a maverick makes his way up, they'll either move over a little for him or break him; that's what the institution is set up for. But he can't make his way up unless he plays the game by the rules. The system can only be drastically modified if an actual new power-base makes the scene.

If we're convinced that an actual demonic violence has infiltrated the Establishment, we know we can't fight it from inside. But society is bigger than the State. The ultimate weapon of the State is its propaganda about its own importance. When we lift off the propaganda, we find the reality: a group of men operating it with ruthlessness, perhaps brilliance, for their own purposes—which are fatally unexamined and short-sighted. We can learn from them. Any radical threat to the Establishment must be of the same nature: a counter-organization of persons.

There's only one system of political and economic power, and they monopolize it. We must move into the unoccupied territory. Where they operate by mutual personal interest, we must operate by mutual acceptance of ideology. Where they persuade by blackmail and bribery, we must persuade by argument and participation. Where they control by manipulation of the media, we must control by actual representation of the oppressed. *The only effective counter-organization to an exploitative Establishment is a voluntary community of principle.*

The Soviet Union isn't all that different from the United States. Their rulers and ours are in some kind of collusion which they call détente, and are developing parallel bureaucracies. Especially they're agreed that there's an important difference between us and them constituted by our economic sysems. It's a defensive smoke-screen to ask which large-scale economic system will best promote primary individual rights. The real issue is whether any large-scale economic system will do this. As we become less and less impressed with the difference between Capitalism and Communism, we cry for a system which isn't administered from a long ways away but is really responsive to our local wishes. We haven't the power in our hands to plan a massive reshaping of society for the better; neither, quite obviously, do they. We can set up fragments of a counter-organization to reshape it locally: farmer co-ops, consumer co-ops, free universities, free Churches, volunteer orchestras, baby-sitting centers, rent strikes, tutoring bureaus—community organization. This mayn't take us very far but at least it's ours. At the same time we'll try and find a prophetic and creative way of dealing with the gross violence done by the system at the center.

The great thing is not to take the Establishment at its own estimate. Its showy electoral process isn't the scene of decision, the alleged competitive economic system isn't the scene of control, the mass media aren't the scene of thought. Instead we turn to the reality of the Establishment, a community of persons. We turn its ideology upside down, following the clues given by the Gospel, and begin working for renewal wherever it's possible. Positive avenues of rebuilding at first are scarce. For the moment the principal job is the resisting of violence. Voluntary organization through true community of interest is the only permanent scene where we can do either.

If we try to start a new voluntary community from scratch we get into the bag of definition, ambition, publicity. Better if we can find a community already existing, however corrupt or fossilized, with the desired ideology built in. History provides us with a ready-made community which was the original point of emergence for reconciliation: the Church. Besides the organizational problem of liberating it into conformity with its own definition, history provides us with a theoretical problem in utilizing it: the language in which it defines its own nature. The heart of that language, and of our linguistic problem, is the divine names in ancient books. In the next chapter I suggest that they're the best label we could ask for to paste on our own current understanding of things.

I

IV

SPEAKING ABOUT GOD

1. The grammar of wisdom

(a) The analysis of language

A living language may be learned by an adult just so far as he can become a leader in the society that speaks it. From even the rare authors who learned English as adults something is lacking. In Conrad we miss the rhythms that a child gets from its mother; Nabokov is too absorbed in that prattle. The deeper we're dyed in our mother's language, with all its excellences and limitations, the more human we are.

Grammar is a real science because its subject is inexhaustible. We keep going back to old texts for fresh light. Not so with even the greatest mathematical work, a *Principia:* later generations can translate it into an improved symbolism with increase of elegance, and leave nothing unaccounted for. But where mathematics is our servant, words are our masters. Humpty Dumpty was kidding himself; when we use a word it *doesn't* mean just what we choose it to mean, neither more nor less. If I write "lion," "emerald," "consul," it means what *it* chooses to mean. Gold goes beyond the conventional realms of the physicist or the banker; its permanence makes it a universal symbol of the eternal realm, and if "gold" loses that sense, the word has simply failed in its duty of bringing the whole thing before us. I'm at liberty to assemble a critical mass of plutonium or of words; what happens then depends on the nature of things, not on my wishes.

Grammar is both a theory analyzing what another man's language does, and the applied technique by which we learn to do what *our* circumstances call for. Since a literary text is the deposit of a whole society, the tent of grammar has to stretch over the whole three-ring circus. It must be a science, like physics or biology, which begins to grasp a real developing whole. And we're not entitled to select our own data, stepping on the bugs that don't fit the classification; we have to accept things as they come.

(b) The death of "God"

Nobody can expand his mind to all contemporary forms of expression. My habits of thinking square prevent me from writing hippie. If I train myself to switch out of one medium into another, I lose the rare strength in a Thucydides or Milton of bending all matter to one uniquely appropriate style. Actual choices have to be made—some for us before we're born. Much less can we necessarily count on handling features of past language. "Thou art" is hardly available any longer. We who are just losing our last subjunctives to modal auxiliaries, our last case-endings, wonder how it would feel to think in subjunctive *and* optative, or in eight cases. English (we say) breaks down into simple undeclinable parts the notion which Greek or Arabic expresses by a single complex verb-form. But how far is translation really possible? When English develops two words, literal "sky" and figurative "heaven," it can't do justice to languages with only one word always possessing both connotations. It's not the case that words have a "literal" meaning which is the mother of metaphor. If anything, the opposite; the sky was the abode of Gods before it was an element, and a pretty abstract one, of cosmology.

Another feature of old texts is apparently even more foreign to our own usage, and resistant to paraphrase: the presence of *divine names*, our constant awareness in the texts of God or the Gods. We can't expurgate them or edit them out. Greek tragedy remained a cult performance dedicated to Dionysus; the Gods often appear as actors, and regularly in the ostensible beliefs of the chorus. Hebrew prophecy is words attributed to God in first person or describing his action in third person; Hebrew psalms are addressed to him in second person.

The divine names are special proper nouns with (in each language) a peculiar syntax which suitably distinguishes them from ordinary proper nouns. Some are like personal names of individuals with a well-marked character: Apollo, Aphrodite, Astarte. Greek *theos* is both a common noun to label the class these names belong to, and also serves in *ho theos*, *"the* God," to define any one of them when he's monopolizing our attention. Most Phoenician divine names are really courtesy titles: Adonis "Lord," Baal "Master," Baalat "Mistress." I don't know if the Gods so addressed had real personal names also like Tammuz or Eshmun; maybe they were less distinctly conceived. The unimaginative Romans, before falling under Greek influence, thought of their Gods as associated in colleges, like the priests who served them: Manes "spirits of the dead," Lares and Penates "household Gods," and just plain *di* "Gods." Greek formal civic religion also invokes them collectively, *theoi*. Hebrew *Elohim*, though ostensibly a masculine plural, takes a singular adjective and verb when it's a Hebrew divine name. But it's also the only plural "Gods" that Hebrew possesses. The other principal Hebrew divine name, conventionally written *Yahweh*, came to be so sacred that its true pronunciation was lost. Modern tongues are so far influenced by Israel or Aristotle that they've only got one divine name, like English *God*. It has to serve both as a proper name of the only God now permitted us, and as a class-name (with a small "g" which I raise out of courtesy) for talking about societies more richly endowed.

Nobody can keep in his mind at once the whole spectrum of novelties which have entered history. The Greeks spread their divine sponsors out in space, allotting each God his own sanctuary or aspect of life. The Hebrews operated similarly but in time, replacing each old name or concept as it was rendered irrelevant by history. They began with old Canaanite names, El Elyon ("Most High El") and El Shaddai; then on to Elohim, Yahweh of hosts,

"The Holy One of Israel," and "our Father in Heaven." Mysteriously the end of the evolution is the old Indo-European name,
Jupiter the sky-father. And we still apply Greco-Roman terms,
"theology" and "divinity," to the Hebrew tradition.

Language, which grew up along with social structure as its
mirror, is a geological deposit of our whole history. Archaic modes
of feeling and thinking, above all in the use of the divine names,
persist fossilized into the present; they're concentrated at the two
ends of the social spectrum, among the least and the most educated.
On the one hand they appear as unreflective credos ("In God we
trust"), curses ("damn it"), exclamations (*mon Dieu*). Their appeal
is *intentionally* illegitimate, to claim for patriotism, anger, or the
like a sanction in the past which both speaker and hearer recognize
as unfair: "For Christ's sake get out of my way."

Elsewhere the divine names are stranded in the self-conscious
usage of philosophy and theology. Academic persons who speak
about God live by taking in each other's washing; they defend or
attack a proposition invented by somebody else. Anybody who
suggested a radically new proposition about God would be a rarer
bird than an academic—a prophet. Somebody that could invent
new divine names and express important truths through them
would be more than a prophet, perhaps mad; who follows William
Blake?

A contemporary school of theologians, adopting a phrase of
Nietzsche, says that God is dead. By this they seem to mean that
Greek and Hebrew divine language, as it's been translated for us
in English dress, is no longer available for sensitive contemporaries
to express their actual concerns. Some want to agree with what the
New Testament says, but feel that they have to say it a different
way, and that they can. Some disagree with it and want to say
something different. All agree that we can't simply appropriate for
our own use its notions in its language. So far as they're simply
recording the current scene they make good sense: most religious
language at most times, especially the present time, is phony. But
they may be saying, not that they can't learn to speak with the
tradition, but that they won't.

Still in fact, if I find that Aeschylus or Isaiah is the author who

best lights up my own condition, Apollo or Yahweh has already
established a beachhead in my mind, neither as curse nor as metaphysics, but in something like his original function. "You should
say rather that the old names correspond to realities recognized in
our language; but to speak of Apollo or Yahweh yourself is ironical
or archaizing." Irony and archaism necessarily enter our language
whenever we talk about subjects that concern us most; we make
wry comparisons with the beliefs of other people, analogies to the
past. Language can't even be merely straight on the subject of life
or death:

Do not go gentle into that good night.

Initially we may say that the divine names are used precisely to
mark both a continuity and a break with what the past considered
important. "God is dead" marks the break right enough, but not
the continuity; it hasn't yet identified the name in our language of
the things once affirmed, or trusted itself to go and look for it.

(c) Where poets go to school

What philosophers and theologians say today about God can
be traced back (either in agreement or disagreement) to scholasti-
cism and the Christian fathers; thence to the New Testament and
Hebrew poetry on one hand, and to Aristotle and Greek poetry on
the other. But there the genealogical tree stops; Greek and Hebrew
culture seem to have some actual source of information about the
Gods inaccessible to us. It's true the names were taken over by the
Greeks from Anatolian myth and elsewhere, by the Hebrews from
Canaanite cult. But what they say about those names isn't a fossil
embedded in their language; it expresses a massive originality. How
did the ancient poets learn what to say about the Gods? Not from
tradition as with us. Their testimony embarrasses us in its
unanimity: *it was the Gods who taught them!* Their witness isn't
any less or more a literary affectation than when Blake or Milton
or Dante or Vergil also claims to be inspired.

We learn to use the names of the Gods, like other nouns and
parts of speech, from our mother, our brothers and sisters, older

kids in the street, visiting adults. Their language isn't on one level;
it has strata of reminiscence which the child learns to use appropri-
ately, like other strata. As we learn to read, and as our reading goes
wider, the sequence of signs transmits to our inner ear oral recita-
tions by the dead poet superimposed on maternal rhythms. Then
when we read the poetry of a language different from our mother's,
in translation or the original, we begin to learn a second international language, whether as readers or as poets in our own right:
the language of symbol. So painters start from the point reached
by other painters, and scientists from t'.e current state of knowledge. Poets are as learned as possible; they never willingly cut
themselves off from the dimension of meaning generated by a continuous reference to past poets.

The poet doesn't operate with words alone as his units. The
vocabulary of Homer includes nouns with fixed epithets, half lines,
traditional groups of verses. The Hebrew poet works with phrases
which we read now in Canaanite texts of 1400 B.C. from Ugarit;
the scheme of parallel elements in half-verses is fixed by usage, it
recurs from prophet to prophet. The poet works inside an old
comprehensive set of linguistic conventions, not devised by himself, which have always been used for the same purposes. He's been
taught that skill in that medium is the key to a realm of primary
meaning.

Ancient texts aren't exactly the product of human intelligence
working on given materials; rather they're the given materials
which constitute a culture. The ancient poets looked on their craft
as the scientist does on his, whatever each knows about its history:
as a concentrated summary of important truths which no one man
could have worked out by himself. In fact, modern science and
modern poetry are two things that have come out from that once
indivisible enterprise.

The ancient texts which introduce God, or the Gods, regularly
state that they go beyond us. As the heavens are higher than the
earth, so are Yahweh's ways higher than our ways; the races of men
and of Gods are one and the same, but the brazen sky lies between.
"How can the poet's human language claim to control something
which he sees only dimly?" The language isn't his, it belongs to the

Gods. "But language is simply one way of representing our experience in human society." Among the things we experience in human society are the systems of organized energy once called Gods. For the Greeks (as Walter Otto says), "Dionysus" was the name of a shared experience cutting across all the recognized forms of political life, involving drunkenness, madness, ecstasy, identification with animals and with nature, inspiration, dismemberment. Poetry, and our deepest experiences which it records, are the invasion of society and personality by what we best describe as an outside force.

The poets testify that what they sing isn't their creation, but comes from some source other than their personality. No grammatical programming can exhaust a language, because each poet is the scene of innovation. He picks up, blowing in the wind, scraps of lines, hints of the future, laborers' sayings, observations of nature; and more by receptivity than willpower lets them put themselves in a suitable order. We know he didn't invent the language, the vocabulary, the idioms. No more did he invent the poem; it wouldn't strike home to people unless all those items were in their experience also. In strict law all copyright should be vested in the Muse. In the poet is crystallized the precise utterance for which history was supersaturated. Thus the text comes at us with an advance claim on our trust. It says what we already know and more; or what we already knew without realizing it. From that initial trust we take on credit expressions that seem opaque or freaky; if later on they too light up, we realize we've found a guide to our experience. Wisdom has touched our ear.

(d) Approaching ancient texts

We approach contemporary texts out of our own experience. We approach ancient texts out of history, acquiring as much as possible of the information available to contemporaries. After we've informed ourselves as best we can, the clue to those texts is a *grammar of wisdom*. The way a Greek or Hebrew expressed himself is the original mode of defining what it means to be a man. And the heart of the definition is the fact of expressing oneself; man is a mirror-making animal. There isn't any general agreement that more modern forms of words have rendered the old obsolete. The burden of proof is on the person who claims the ancient texts have been superseded; they come with a general presumption in their favor. In particular, we're to presuppose until the opposite is proved that the divine names are performing an important function.

Linguistic analysts start from modern philosophy rather than from ancient texts; and not even from actual books of modern philosophy, but from artificial sentences expressing what the analyst thinks the philosophers ought to say. "God is an omniscient omnipotent being." This doesn't have the rhythm of a language actually spoken, nor the allusiveness of the poet. But those features of old texts are essential to any kind of speaking about God. By inspecting the meaning (or lack of meaning) in sentences like this, we haven't yet gotten close to the actual language about God which has moved people to action.

If those writers saw the world of human experience for the first time, it's worth a try to project ourselves into their mind—in particular, not stiffening the divine names into a dogmatic scheme of our own which we father on them. It's my experience that all poetry which moves me is talking about the same thing:

> There is one story and one story only
> That will prove worth your telling . . .

What's the most accurate way of saying that thing? We're suspicious when a novelist intrudes his personal Communism or Catholicism, because we're sure that current forms of those beliefs are cruder instruments than his own perceptions. A form of belief which would lead the author to truths he'd otherwise have missed seems scarcely possible to us, but is taken for granted by the ancient world.

The philologist can expound the ancient texts containing the divine names. Priests can give contemporary renditions of those texts treated as liturgy. Uneducated persons and philosophers use the names vestigially in their own language. But a living use of the divine names is possible today only for poets operating in their own right inside the old grammar of wisdom. Unlike other features of language, use of the divine names can't ever be merely conventional; they only exist inside creative discourse. Thus every man has the potentiality of becoming a poet himself, using words properly to go with his actions.

We've seen that the problem which the philosopher calls "the existence of God" is more correctly the function of the divine names in ancient texts. We will discover that the center of their use is to affirm the emergence of radical novelties into history. As poets or prophets in our own right, we're entitled and required to follow their style; and in particular to affirm that God is responsible for the loving revolution in Jesus—just as the New Testament affirms it. The affirmation of love is hollow without joy—which in turn requires a victory over death. But nonviolence is precisely the thing which death can't touch; the joyfulness implied by its attribution to God is self-vindicating.

2. The presence of divine names in ancient texts

(a) The claim of the Gods on us

Literary criticism of ancient texts—as carried out both by the classical scholar and the biblical theologian—informs us of the function of the divine names. The ancient poets agree in regarding the words which have passed through them as *revelation*. The role of the biblical text in the Church of course continues this self-estimate of the poets; equally so the role of classical literature in Western education.

The Church and the Synagogue used to take the Hebrew Bible at face value, seeing the law of Moses as primary, the prophets as secondary exegesis. With our historical methods, we reverse the roles: the prophets from Amos on made an original response to a crisis of violence which was then projected back onto the mythical lawgiver. (New Testament scholars naturally but wrongly tried to make the same reversal. It's true that we have Paul's letters in earlier form than the Gospels. But, where Moses is a blank for us, it's Jesus who represents the original spiritual impulse which Paul interprets and adapts.) During the Renaissance, Latin literature and sculpture were seen as normative, and things Greek as stiff primitive forerunners. The radical originality of the Greeks was first appreciated by nineteenth-century German scholarship and archaeology. Not until World War II did we get English translations of Greek drama able to stand beside the King James Bible. Far from the classical world being superseded, not until our generation could it have the same effect on contemporaries as the English Bible on Bunyan.

If Greek and Hebrew societies are really two foci of a single movement, then the culture of the city-state, divine names and all, presents us with more of an ultimatum than we thought. We've got to take or leave the whole package.We thought we could discard biblical religion while retaining Greek literary values. But then our reading of the Bible as literature made the same kind of claims for it. The Gods have their hooks in us deeper than we recognized.

Neither body of texts separates people into insiders who accept it and outsiders who don't. Precisely the claim of Athens and Jerusalem to be schools of humanity is the fact that they arrange pre-enrollment for alleged outsiders. At the same time, important information about our place in the cosmos may be obtained from American Indian or African oral literature, Hindu or Chinese books. We have an urgent duty to immerse ourselves deeply enough in those cultures that we can begin to make a comparison. The historical parts of this book are intended to make some sense out of *our* tradition.

(b) The Gods as makers and sustainers

Ancient man—our one primary source of information—sees the Gods as both *starting* things, and *maintaining* what they once started. The act by which Adam was created brings each of us Adams also into being. The Hebrew God preserves the world from being dissolved by waves of chaos just as he first created it. The Greek Gods still preside over the element which they originally received by lot. On the acropolis of every city-state stood the protecting temple of the God under whose auspices it was founded. The legend of the past act—dragon-combat, shaping of man, exodus, city-planning—is read as libretto of the dramatic liturgy through which its impetus is celebrated and maintained in the present.

This double view of the divine activity corresponds to how things actually are. The absolute novelties of past evolution are deployed in the present as the relative novelty of birth and development in each individual. Who taught my children their duty of having an Easter egg hunt? Recapitulation, biological and historical, is the Time-machine which brings the evolutionary content of the past living before our eyes. History is swung around at right angles into geological and social strata; time is spatialized in organic structures.

The sciences, natural and social, train us in the habit of seeing those past emergents built into the present. But eventually freedom must push us out of contemplation into action. Nature and society take thought for reproducing the whole sequence of past evolution in us. *Our* job is to affirm the action by which the radical novelty of the future surfaces, claiming the kinship with the Gods that constitute our humanity. The divine power is more itself when it starts something than when it's just maintaining it. We see the finger of the Gods at the precise point where the cotyledons of the future break through our soil.

(c) Some texts with the divine names

A. Isaiah 43:18-19 (R.S.V.):

> Remember not the former things,
>   nor consider the things of old.
> Behold, I am doing a new thing;
>   now it springs forth, do you not perceive it?
> I will make a way in the wilderness
>   and rivers in the desert.

B. Pindar, *Olympian* iii.1-5 (trans. Richmond Lattimore):

> My claim is to sing bright Akragas and please the Tyndaridai,
>   the lovers of strangers,
> and their sister Helen with the splendid hair,

shaping the hymn of Olympic triumph for Theron, the speed
    of his horses
with feet never weary. So the Muse was near as I found a fire-
    new style
to set in the Dorian cast the speech
    of acclamation . . .

C. Paul, to the Galatians 4:3-7:

So we also, when we were children, were enslaved under
the elemental principles (*or*, ABC's) of the cosmos. But
when the fulness of time came, God sent forth his Son, born
of a woman, born under the Law, so that he might buy back
those who were under the law, so that we might receive
adoption. And because you are sons, God sent the Spirit of
his Son into your hearts, crying *Abba*, "Father." So you are
no more a slave, but a son; and if a son, then an heir through
God.

D. Blake, *Jerusalem* folio 77:

England! awake! awake! awake!
    Jerusalem thy Sister calls!
Why wilt thou sleep the sleep of death
    And close her from thy ancient walls?

Thy hills and valleys felt her feet
    Gently upon their bosoms move:
Thy gates beheld sweet Zion's ways:
    Then was a time of joy and love.

And now the time returns again:
    Our souls exult, and London's towers
Receive the Lamb of God to dwell
    In England's green and pleasant bowers.

The sacred bards move with assurance, as in their own house,
in a spiritual geography peopled with figures not exactly human:

Jerusalem, Olympia, England; Helen, the Muse, Yahweh, the
Son of God. That landscape or seascape with figures is stirring into
action: *the God is bringing something new into being.*

Our poets are all speaking about the mystery of time. The
movements of peoples: the matter of Britain, the calling of Israel,
the possibility of Athens. Our texts at their most mythical see
realities far better than the cyclic theory which Aristotle imposes
on his elegant biological observations. Men living in a time of rapid
social change have the best clue to the nature of things in general,
if they'll use it.

All these poets were in fact conscious of history being on the
march. Deutero-Isaiah and Pindar were nearly contemporaries;
they worked under the influence of Persian expansion, and the
blossoming of the city-state into the new thing we've discussed. The
Hebrew envisages the return from exile, the refounding of Israel;
the Greek celebrates the victories of Sicilian lords over barbarism.
Paul has been so overwhelmed by the novelty of Jesus, that he's
pushed into this shattering myth which affronts us still by its
audacity and humorlessness. Blake, in the face of Deism and the
Industrial Revolution, and in touch with the Wesleyan revival, sees
on the horizon the Romantic movement—and a renewal of England for which he's the best witness. All these texts are the best
evidence that a new spirituality has happened; by "Romanticism"
we *mean* primarily a body of poetry.

These are about the simplest texts I could find. Yahweh elsewhere performs more extensive actions than our prophet speaks of
here, many of which (like the genocide of the Canaanites) we
rightly choose not to swallow. All together they cover the whole
trajectory of global history and individual life. Pindar, in spite of
his complicated technique, takes the Gods straighter than Greek
drama or Job, with their oblique viewpoint and ambiguities. Paul's
imitators make us forget that no primary thinker has expressed
thoughts remotely like his; we have only a fragment of the myth
here. Dante and Milton are thought bigger poets than Blake—but
less original; his passages show a very rare simplicity in inventing
a new myth out of old materials. The manifest power of these texts

needs no defense; it'll take the linguistic analysts a long time to describe what's happening in them.

(d) Convention and novelty in the use of divine names

In Greek literature, epic is a precocious Enlightenment, where the Gods appear as a sideshow, and the poet's serious business is men. (Perhaps Homer, a Mycenaean refugee, found that his Gods got weaker away from their native soil—just as Naaman the Syrian did.) Serious discourse about the Gods is localized in the mainland farmer Hesiod, the orthodox lyricists Sappho and Pindar, and the dramatists on their home ground of Attica. In tragedy the Gods are not so much Olympian as of the earth, earthy. Comedy is the most ambivalent of media, and the ingenious fun that Aristophanes makes of the Gods has a more serious look than Homer's. There are doubtless elements of literary convention also in the use of the Gods by Aeschylus or Sophocles—that's why they don't offend us. But the same could then be said of T. S. Eliot. If divine names everywhere represent a literary convention, a "literary convention" is just the way books are written, we are then freed to analyze the function of the words as we find them.

The alternatives of conventional belief and unbelief seem strongly inappropriate in the face of these texts. One feels recognition and hope: a catch in the throat that after so many disappointments, a more exciting thing than we felt any right to wish for is on its way. The proper content of the living present must be some overwhelming novelty.

Even in these relatively simple texts, the divine persons and places are shadowed with ambiguity. Blake is talking about the arrival of Mediterranean culture in Britain. It would have been very impertinent to ask Blake if he really believed the Hebrews came originally from "Albion"; and his answer would have been impertinent. How seriously does Pindar take the apparently external character of his lady Muse? The manner in which Yahweh goes about road-building isn't very clearly conceived. And has Paul worked out the details of the trans-historical affair in which the Father sends the Son?

We could as well have gathered antithetical visions of approaching evil. Here even more we'd find that the affirmations can't ever be straight—they have a necessary sardonic quality. We won't get a clear answer either if we ask whether Pindar believes in the dragon Typhon or not. He certainly believes in the existence of barbarian disorder which the dragon symbolizes. Likewise if we ask whether Deutero-Isaiah believes in Leviathan (same dragon!), or whether he's just using it as a Canaanite literary allusion. Observe the characteristic irony that Jesus applies to Beelzebul, who exists primarily in somebody else's world of belief rather than in ours. That doesn't mean we don't need him. If he didn't exist he'd have to be invented—with the peculiar attributes of non-being which in fact invest him.

Traditionally philosophers have asked: Are sentences like those of our texts meaningful? Do the divine names in them have some equivalent in reality? If meaningful, are these sentences also true? But actually we should ask: What are the sentences *doing?* What function do the divine names serve in them? By muting the divine symbolism we could translate Greek tragedy into a realistic novel or play. Thucydides did precisely this; he paraphrased its brooding horror into actual history. It might seem to reflect on the status of the Gods if they can be translated away: equally, however, it reflects on the enterprise of Thucydides if his rationalism is only a literary choice. A literary choice must be a more serious decision than we thought.

Which literary choice is more normal, more effective? In *King Lear*, redemption is generated out of blindness, war, thunderstorms —not all that different from saying that Yahweh generates redemption from the cloud over Sinai. But Shakespeare's technique is more difficult to pull off, more sophisticated. The divine names have a more long-standing claim as label for the reality. Yahweh and Zeus work well precisely because they have a long handle in the past. Scholars know that "Zeus" is an Indo-European name for the sky; Isaiah will have us think back to the legend in which the name "Yahweh" was revealed to Moses. All these elements of association, archaism, ambiguity, are necessary for the normal functioning

K

of the divine names. Unambiguous language hasn't enough tensile strength to bear the load of the Gods.

3. God and the Gods as source of innovation

(a) Deciding to use the divine names

The divine names appear normally as subjects of verbs, which express the emergence of radical novelty in the living present, continuous with remote beginnings. *Yahweh* is plausibly interpreted as an archaic causative participle of the verb *to be*, "he who brings to pass." This is why the divine names aren't among the features of language which get old and unusable, like "thou art" and "if it be." Their function requires them to be self-renewing— they define the self-renewing of the universe.

This function of divine names in ancient texts corresponds to the shape we found in ancient history. We saw the meaning of the city-state as the birth of twins—freedom and violence. From the death of the city-state came the transformation of freedom into love —the emergence of a liberated community which didn't need to be protected any longer by the defenses around its birth. The ancients saw the meaning of their own history just as clearly as we do, or better. And the best way they could explain the possibility of that history was to say that the Gods did it.

Yahweh, in a long series of events, is seen as creating the universe, the society of man, the nation Israel, the city Jerusalem. Then, partly in punishment for sin, partly in fulfillment of destiny, he breaks down the walls and leads the people out into the world under the banner of his Servant. Each time the action is seen as a narrow escape from drowning, a passage through watery chaos. The Gods lead out the Achaean armies against Troy, and induce a poet to record the campaign. Pindar sees them as presiding each over his own international temple—Zeus at Olympia, Apollo at Delphi—and supervising the destinies of individual states. Aeschylus has the intervention of Athena break the chain of bloodguilt. In Prometheus and Oedipus a divine figure suffering outside the city wall is the instrument of redemption for society. Socrates gave the credit for his "wisdom" to his *daimonion*. We saw how earlier history rolled itself up into a ball in the life of Jesus, the supreme emergent. We need now only observe that Paul, the Evangelists, and (with all ambiguities) Jesus himself agree in holding God responsible for the revolution he embodies.

Are we justified in using the divine names to talk about the things that matter most? (Paul affirms that we're justified *by* using them.) The element of linguistic convention in their use does not go beyond the original linguistic convention involved in using language at all. It's not true that metaphor, irony, association, form a decorative level of language imposed on a more basic literal level. The farther back we go in the Western tradition, the more allusive and sacred the texts become. A purely secular use of language— what we may call prose—is the most sophisticated and fragile of civilized achievements.

I can't dissociate myself from the words used by the past. As our embryology recapitulates biological evolution, we may add that *our psychological development recapitulates history*. Today my personal development and our common history have reached the same point, and for a few years will proceed along together, until I slacken and the torch is picked up by somebody else. We bypass stages in our development at our own risk, and only if we can find an adequate substitute. Marxism is thought an heir to the Gods; but Jesus reached his position precisely by repudiating revolutionary violence. The Johnson era should have discredited the belief in automatic progress for all time—while at the same time vindicating the power of moral concern to change the actual course of history.

In Chapter III we decided that, not as moral ideal but as enlightened prudence, the revolutionary nonviolence of Jesus was indicated by our own circumstances as the course to follow. We're now at the point where we see every reason to affirm the things he stood for *in his own words*: to make the language of divine names *our* language. At first this won't seem to affect anything but the style of our affirmations. The grammar of wisdom teaches us to use the divine names in the same way as our best models. In that case there won't be any occasion to talk about the attributes of God in himself, as distinct from his innovating activity in history; that would be inappropriate syntax.

But the style of our affirmations makes all the difference. We can only use the divine names in the spirit of prophecy. The traditional syntax also forbids our involving the divine names in a *prosaic* context. Religion, Tillich says, is our ultimate concern. Religious language is talk about our ultimate concern. If it doesn't sound like ultimate concern it's not religion. And that involves using such words as really bring the heart of a man before his neighbor. This is the level on which the divine names operate. So they turn out not to be fossil dinosaurs, but permanently youthful Giants, even if for the most part today asleep or on a journey. We haven't got any other poetry but existing poetry to work with; we'll use the language which has been given us, or none. Of course, it must be with our own innovations, but still within the tradition. Our liberation is to reach out for the only tool which will do the job. The divine names are the only language available to say the thing that has to be said. We had better grasp the nettle.

(b) The activity of God

God is revolution, a revolution which goes beyond the most characteristic revolutions we know in not letting itself become contaminated with the thing it's revolting against. Actually, in saying this I'm still talking about the divine names—the "attributes of God in himself"—not quite yet about the living reality. What I should have said was: God *makes* revolution. I use "revolution" as Jesus used "Kingdom of God," because these are the political terms which move contemporaries most deeply, and man is a political animal. Radicals and reactionaries are alike proud to be called sons and daughters of the American Revolution.

This formula simply generalizes "In the beginning God created the heavens and the earth . . ." The fact that cosmic evolution takes place at all is a revolutionary emergence out of the nonbeing which is all we could imagine by ourselves. We can now go back through our previous analysis, picking up the successive phases of historic change and talking about them in the language we're newly privileged to speak. The ultimate version of revolution is the radical nonviolence of Jesus. It hasn't got anything common with the system of violence it overthrows.

The Civil Rights revolution, the Peace revolution, the inarticulate cry for a Conservation revolution—these massive facts of our time (we've now learned to say) are the work of God. As usual, he's picked the outcast to shame and if possible convert the elder brother. Perhaps both alleged outsiders and alleged insiders will become suspicious at this point. Does this equivalence between the best ancient and the best modern language lead the outsider into the bag of affirming a supernatural being, or the insider into the desert of secularism by false identifications? There's absolutely no basis for dividing people into outsiders and insiders. *People who see clearly and act responsibly must somehow all be affirming one and the same world.* What keeps us from speaking about that world in the same way must be the shortness of our life, the difficulty of the matter, sin, and a bad educational system. But if we're ever to have reconciliation with our enemies we've got to find a way of getting along with our friends. I'm trying to suggest how people who're moved by the same books and respond to the same needs can speak in the same language—which after all was meant to be a bridge.

(c) The finality of the revolution in Jesus

Orthodoxy has always held that the new thing in Jesus was the final revelation. But how can the pattern of successively emergent novelties, which up until now has been labeled "time," ever come to a halt? Can God modify his habit of making revolution? The new principle represented by Jesus lends itself to such general formulation (namely, the way he originally expressed it) that it's hard to see how it could ever be superseded. It refuses to carve out a domain other than the domain of the Cross, which is always open. He allows every truly natural growth—lilies, ravens, children, laborers—to flourish in the ecological niche where God has placed them. When the violence of competition for niches enters, he holds up the mirror of truth to both parties and asks them to reexamine their motives. It turns out to be those closest to himself, the poor, who, if anybody, shove over and let violence work itself out. In a universe of apparently fixed volume and finite resources, what other means of permanently resolving territorial disputes can there be?

By making this means available, he brings a whole new dimension of psychic space into the universe, which the poor then inherit. What novelty could be looked for after this?

Jesus is the turning point of history. The subsequent revolutions we may look forward to will be the application of nonviolence to new areas. A large field—just about everywhere—still remains to be won over. The revolution we can expect in our own time is the transformation of a worldwide Established Church (the state Churches of Western powers and their missions overseas) into something which hasn't ever existed before: a worldwide Church on the model of the primitive one, everywhere associating itself with the hopes of the poor.

This analysis perhaps makes it again possible for us to talk about the presence of God in history. If we live our lives inside the rhythm of history, as we should, his presence spills over into them too. But how can we go on affirming his activity so far as *we're* concerned, when our date with history is scrubbed by death? To finish the rehabilitation of language about God, we still must find a way to affirm the old formula that in him death has been overcome.

4. Nonviolence as guarantee of the resurrection

(a) Coming to terms with our death

Our awareness of violence in every form is intensified by death. We can't with a quiet mind turn over to our children an environment which we've run somewhat more downhill, or set them in an unjust social arrangement, whether as masters or slaves. At just the point when they become fully engaged in the struggle against injustice, they let us slip away into the undignified senior-citizen arrangements of our broken society. Under the best of circumstances death is the final act of violence against our personality. Today the general crisis of violence is internalized as the fear of death in well-known particular symbolic forms.

Language about God isn't a present indicative statement that something is going on. The presence of the divine names makes it subjunctive, investing it with the affirmation that everything in some manner should be seen as good. The past revolutions recapitulated in us, the present one which in our freedom we help bring to light, should let us rest easy in the conviction that we're at home in the cosmos which generated us. But the crushing legacy of violence won't let us. We can't claim full citizenship in the cosmos by birthright; naturalization is required. To take language about God seriously, we must come to terms with the violence summed up in our death.

The Greeks (a clear-sighted people whose ideology fitted their feelings) never became reconciled to dying. So their Gods are bugged by death too: they're not all-powerful to preserve us from it, they also are subject to humiliation. For a long time the Hebrews could avoid facing up to death, because they maintained a traditional society where men lived vicariously in their children. When it broke down, Yahweh had to be granted increased power—it was too late to take on Greek realism. That increased power is the raising of the dead, which is first affirmed for the martyred Maccabean freedom fighters. But at that point the Jews didn't fully believe in the Resurrection—a fanatical extra which couldn't generate the required spirituality. So Jesus came into a world doubly hung up on death, in the symbolic form of hysterical incapacities seen as demonic powers.

Since Jesus and Paul lived in a crisis of violence like ours, the boundlessness of their affirmations about God forced them to hold radically that the death at the heart of violence had been overcome. They didn't have any choice but to make the inherited image of resurrection central. The plastic character of New Testament symbolism was bound to produce narratives of an actual resurrection-event, whether it happened or not. Paul or Luke could hardly have fathered on the primitive Christian communities a belief they didn't share. We may take the New Testament at face value: the deposit of a brotherhood which had passed beyond fear of death.

Jesus emphasizes the conditions for appropriating the victory over death; they constitute the style of life which we've called revolutionary nonviolence. Now this original mode of thought and conduct is the one actual new thing which has entered the picture, to change the clear-sighted pessimism of the Greek city, the unreal fanaticism of the Maccabees, into the affirmation of joy in the primitive Church. So we conclude that *the will to practice nonviolent reconciling love must somehow lie at the base of hope in the resurrection.*

Perhaps it seemed as if the question, "But does God really exist?" was dispensed with by grammatical tricks. When we leave the realm of public history behind, and ask how the question really comes at us, it always reduces to one existential translation: "Have I still grounds for hope in face of the certainty of my death?" For resurrection is always seen as the action of God alone.

(b) Our solidarity with the human race

If once we're persuaded on some level that the nonviolent revolution is the right way, we immediately know we fall short of it. It's easy enough to see the things out there arrayed against us: affluence; the military Establishment; the easy natural relations between the Church Establishment and the government; the ease with which awkward moralists can be edged out of the way, their powerlessness in not having any second string to their bow; our tendency to be pushed into ineffectual corners; our propensity to become casualties. All this, we tell ourselves, could be brushed aside if we had such a voice as Paul or Luther or John Wesley or Martin Luther King. But we know in our hearts that we don't. It's not merely that sin has intervened; also we think science has intervened. We feel we know too much about the conditions needed to support consciousness. That is, we haven't enough effectual confidence in God to appropriate what we've been told about his victory over death. The only way is to ask more seriously, more scientifically, what it means to be a man.

Death dissolves both our physical organism and the center of consciousness which it sustained—or perhaps, which sustained it. We saw that consciousness must have some equivalent in every arrangement of matter: when I die, the general principle I represent won't be lost from the universe. But what about the *particular* center of consciousness I represent? We're surer than we should be that we understand what we mean by talking about "my" individuality. Even when I'm stranded on a Polynesian island or rocketed into space, my consciousness keeps a connection with both the biology of the species and human society.

(1) *With the biology of the species.* How does the amoeba feel about undergoing binary fission? Probably uncomfortable. Still, if we can project down to its rudimentary level of consciousness, it's basically immortal. Its consciousness can't be very individualized, since it can split in two without sinking to an enormously more primitive level. I was once on precisely its level. In the human family tree, consciousness rises to the level which I trust my readers are now enjoying, then sinks to the amoebic level of more-than-sleep in the sperm and the ovum. In the chain of our begetting, biological life is continuous, perhaps most intense of all in the sperm and the ovum. And the *fact* of consciousness is continuous —but with sudden drops to near-zero *intensity* when our consciousness humbles itself to the expulsion of living seed. Sexual intercourse is a kind of radical simplification or death—perhaps this may help reconcile us to death.

(2) *With society.* Society isn't maintained by biological descent but by cultural descent: the new mode of genetics which characterizes the universe when it's not merely arranged as biology but also as history. Babies deprived of their mother or a mother-substitute for a long period have lost some essential item of socialization in their makeup which can't be replaced. Other people are a fundamental necessary feature of our consciousness; this isn't moralizing but bare description. We're so conscious of our consciousness when we're alone—reading or writing or walking in the woods—we forget it's dependent on other people. And then we complain about being orphans in the universe, that it pays no attention to us when we die! But our illusion of independence and our outrage at being abandoned are the inside and outside of a pseudo-consciousness.

The same illusion of autonomy leads to social contract theories. But in fact men don't get together and create society; it's the womb within which individual consciousness arose as a focus of group-relations. Language is the symbolic area where man acts most like himself. And linguistic utterance, we know, is the meeting-place of two or more consciousnesses—which then exist only by their participation in this and other kinds of overlap.

(c) What survives death

Most Christians who believe in survival of anything believe in Plato's immortality. But it won't work. It's a distortion of the New Testament, which occurred because in the first centuries of the Church some Platonic philosophers became Christians. They read about the resurrection of the body, couldn't understand it, and explained it in their own terms. If we start taking away from ourselves everything we owe to our bodies, we end up with nothing. The same thing happens if we take away what we owe to other people. Robinson Crusoe isn't simply operating off memories of other people; their connections with him are still operative in his personality—unless that's what we mean by "memory." We haven't got any such thing as Plato's soul, a simple indestructible bit of divine essence; rather the consciousness of each of us is the center of a network of connections.

But by the same token, we haven't got any such thing as the old-fashioned psychologist's self, a simple *destructible* bit of a peculiar substance. So far as one person is genuinely the bond of unity between others, he doesn't die completely or right away. Much more so are poets, physicists, musicians, judges—servants of an ongoing discipline—perpetuated by their consciousness being taken up into an eternal body of knowledge. Even more so when we come to participation in the kind of principle that a man is radically identified with, not merely as father or teacher or artist, but just as himself. Beyond the physical organism, the thing which we *know* will die at our death is our little peculiarities or eccentricities. How important are they? Important to us we say. Should they be? Which things should we feel badly over the death of? We don't feel badly over the death of an individual lion; it's the species lion we've got a psychic stake in. I once said I felt badly about the death of the brontosaurus, but I don't think I do now; I'm satisfied with knowing they once lived, and the time for all that is gone.

We sometimes say the most important part of us is what can

be transmitted or shared. What about Socrates can die? James Bevel said,

I was in Cleveland when someone came running up and said, "We just got a call, A. J. [Muste] is dead." And I said, "Whoever is starting rumors about A. J. being dead must also have started that rumor about God."

I met A. J. up in the office a night or so after he came back from Hanoi. Now, most of us have excuses: you know, "I'm tired, I'm old, I can't do it right now, how about tomorrow?" But that old man stayed up almost the whole night writing up a call for the Spring Mobilization. He was working, involved, giving everything he had, to say to the people of the world, "You are brothers." And most of us half his age get worried we're going to get old and starve to death. That's why most of us don't get anything done; we're sitting around scheming how we're going to get more money, more clothes in our closets, thinking we're going to be naked tomorrow . . .

You see, he understood, and Gandhi understood, and Jesus understood—that all men should be brothers; that they should live together in peace. A. J. went around trying to remove the barriers that separate men. When he was in Hanoi he had the courage to say to Ho Chi Minh, as he said to Johnson in America, "You know something? I've got good news; you guys are brothers. And you shouldn't go around murdering children. That won't solve your problems." . . . We say A. J. is dead and the tragedy is that most of us don't understand the process of life. We say that A. J. is dead but anybody who was caught up in the process of bringing people together can never die. A. J.'s not dead. People working; people creating; people trying to get people together so we can end the war: that's A. J. He isn't dead.

Perhaps somebody so much committed to a principle seems inhuman. Even though A. J. liked baseball very well, he's threatening to the outsider. Is this impersonality or more than personality? We may actually have to make up our minds. Anyway, we can say A. J. was a saint: somebody who translates the style of Jesus into his own style. Jesus invented the character which considers itself unimportant. He certainly was a poet; but he turned his poems over to the memory of his friends, unconcerned with whether they preserved the exact text or original language. By trusting his friends to convey a fair impression of him, he transferred his personality to their safekeeping. By being all of a piece he systematically shrugged off peculiarities. Nothing about a person like that can die. The words and actions, the new principle of nonviolent revolution, the new style which he invented and illustrated, are adequately and completely built into his followers. So Paul says we're in Christ to the extent that we've put off the old man, the wrong principle.

(d) Resurrection as inevitable myth of love

Jesus replaces the counter-productive principle of hanging onto what doesn't matter and must die with the permanence of love. When I find friends, I'm not so certain as I once was whether we're a group of individuals or a collectivity. Totalitarianism is so wicked precisely because it's the perversion of a true pattern. Paul sees the little communities which he calls the Church as representing in embryo the only possible principle of unity in the human race. People have given up their old self-defeating self-affirmation for a new solidarity in coinherence—the context for the only real individualism possible. As in Adam all die, even so in Christ shall all be made alive.

Our habitual categories break down before the novelty of Jesus. Not a myth, like the Saviors of the Oriental religions in the Roman Empire, but a clearly-marked historical person. Nor an abstraction, some idealized proletarian hero. And there wasn't any cult of personality around him: "Why do you call me good?" All the necessary materials to realize the intended nature of humanity were lying around in Palestinian society. By a radical effort of non-self-affirmation he became the catalyst which let them combine into the definitive compound. Rather than call him the true vine, a second Dionysus, I prefer to see in him the colorlessness and tastelessness of water, stating with Pindar that water is best.

He discovered the means built into the human psyche, and implicit in the structure of the universe, by which everything important about us is automatically removed to a realm exempt from death. Nonviolent reconciliation is precisely the thing pointed to in the symbolism of the Resurrection. Nonviolence always has the last word. There's no way of getting round it. It's not idealism or moral advice, but a description, as accurate as possible, of how things actually work. The sting of death is sin. When the alienation between man and man (and between man and nature too) labeled "sin" is overcome, the sting of death is simultaneously withdrawn.

This result is an unexpected dividend from our reaffirmation of the divine names. We suggested in Chapter III that nonviolence was a matter of common sense. We now see that, precisely from the standpoint of orthodox Christianity (the religion which produced the just-war theory!), nonviolence isn't an exceptional individual vocation, but the sole and indispensable requirement for claiming the conquest of death as our own. That doesn't mean it's easy to maintain this confidence in the face of pain, betrayal, separation. But those sufferings are the burden of life; it's death we're trying to deal with.

So far, our view of resurrection has presupposed the continuation of the human species. The patriarchs thought of themselves as living in their actual descendants, the seed of their loins. "Israel" is both the name of a man and of the deathless body of his descendants; so with Greek eponymous ancestors like Ion, the begetter of the Ionians. If like Joseph you've dangled numerous grandsons on your knee, nearly everything important about you is secure. But this traditional way of thinking doesn't survive the expanded need for individual self-fulfillment. At the same time it gives hostages to fortune, on whose behalf we're tempted to violence. Liberation from reliance on this sort of immortality comes by leaving up to Providence who our children are to be—those known or unknown to us who've been influenced by our dream.

If the human race, or life on this planet, comes to an end, such an understanding of resurrection fails also. Teilhard de Chardin was committed to this explanation; he made it an act of faith that the planet couldn't fail until the consummation of humanity (whatever it might be) had been realized. But humanity is an actualization on this planet of something which is a possibility of the space-time

continuum everywhere. There's so much apparent wastage in nature—in the end perhaps not really wastage at all—that we must
face the chance that a younger planet of Gentiles somewhere else
will take over from us if we the elder brother prove unworthy.

All analogy suggests we're not totally cut off from them. Ph.D.
theses are today being written on techniques of interstellar communication. We're told that the whole cosmos travails and groans
together. There's a general principle by which we have as much
contact with other intelligent societies as we need. Columbus was
sent out because it became important for Europe to have America.
The same technology which threatens to destroy the environment
here will reveal whether somebody is doing better elsewhere. A
necessary job of expanding our imagination is being carried out by
science fiction—which however hasn't yet struck its taproot deep
enough through the soil of language to have hit the life-giving water
table of the past.

So far as humanity, or intelligent consciousness anywhere,
goes on in time, love is guarantee of the resurrection, pointing to
the one means by which we can be surest of permanence parallel
to the vector of time. If it fails, all other reliances will have failed
long before. We've learned not to look for fulfillment through territorial expansion along the three dimensions of space surrounding
us. But fulfillment along the time-arrow may itself only be symbolic
of fulfillment in a direction at right angles both to the three space-
dimensions and to time—along a fifth dimension so to speak. In
some moods our poetry affirms that the final scene of permanence
is a quintessential moment where the space-time continuum is as
the mathematician sees it, embedded as a geometric object in a
manifold of higher dimensionality:

> To see a World in a grain of sand
> And a Heaven in a wild flower,
> Hold infinity in the palm of your hand
> And eternity in an hour.

If love is the right thing for us in the moment seen as ephemeral,
much more so in the moment seen as eternal.

This is as far as I can go, or farther, in guessing where survival is. Actually as we know we're not supposed in our analytic geometry so much to give the space-time coordinates of fulfillment as its moral coordinates. Paul next to affirms that the Resurrection has already happened, "So you must consider yourselves dead to sin and alive to God in Christ Jesus." And elsewhere, "We know that we have passed out of death into life, because we love the brethren." The new kind of relationship with our friends is precisely what it means to have overcome death; you can't get a razor blade in between them.

God is responsible for revolution, the principle of innovation. But innovation got turned in on itself by the discovery of love, so that we don't need to expect any more novelties of the same sort. The principle of self-unfolding in the universe is that everything should become its own nature. At first the emergence was done at the cost of some other possibility. The definition of Jesus is that he develops not at somebody else's expense but his own. He's the true Adam; in him human nature is defined as that which prefers other to self. But this is the nature of being generally. He is our naturalization.

As well as I could I've affirmed the historical development of the ancient world, and appropriated its language for ourselves. But the work of Jesus hasn't only come down to us in books bearing his name, and in men and women bearing his name who once read them. It's also come down in a Church bearing his name, more or less illegitimately; and in a wide spectrum of activities for justice and reconciliation which don't bear his name, but are done more or less in his spirit, and which for want of a better name we may call the Movement. If in the face of the crisis of violence we wish to affirm his way, this doesn't yet determine what attitude we should take up to the Church and the Movement. It will be hard to disentangle them from their involvement in the Establishment and in the violent revolution against it. To this problem we now turn.

V

CHURCH RENEWAL AND THE PEACE MOVEMENT

1. The true form of community

(a) The difficulty and strength of community

Establishment power is a network of personal relations—but distorted to do the wrong job. We turn it upside down to restore the ongoing community of love—the least problematical institution. That doesn't mean we can always find it locally realized. Especially in California, enthusiasts are unwilling to take on the professional competence or the sacrifices which would make community practical; they fool around with sexual, psychological, economic experiments. A small intense community gets people so close together that the destructive forces in them are free to interact, and then blows itself apart like a nuclear device by implosion. Community for the sake of community is disastrous. It must exist for the sake of a job to be done, which acts as energy-field to neutralize the forces of repulsion.

That overriding purpose transforms dislikes and frictions by generating an *esprit de corps* where we feel the real strength of our association as the world outside correctly sees it. It's rare for several independent people to surmount the high initial threshold of community. But when they do, it locks them together in hyperstability; the community, like the spiral protein molecules of the gene, organizes the living matter it meets into its own pattern. Hence the tenacity in the nonviolent liberation movements of Danilo Dolci, organizing Sicilian peasants into work-ins, of Gandhi, Cesar Chavez, Martin Luther King. Or we may think of the ecumenical Protestant monasticism of Taizé; the men who are rebuilding the stones and community of Iona; the East Harlem Protestant Parish.

We hold our breath when such a nascent community steps out from the wings of history onto its tightrope. We know that some typical failing, or excess of some virtue, can bring it into either collapse or Establishment fossilization. Still while it's soaring there on its risky course *we understand it.* Most societies at most times fall a long ways short of the true pattern: but we can only say so because sometimes we get a standard of comparison, a community for the time being liberated from the demonic powers. We understand it because its operation is transparent; we hold our breath because we expect communities to be opaque.

(b) The early Churches as continuous with Jesus

The work of Jesus achieved the goal of ancient history: discovering the true form of community. He didn't have any name for it himself. Paul gave the name *ekklesia,* "Church," to any local group claiming that form. Discovering community, like discovering the airplane, involved actually building one. Jesus wasn't merely a prophet but also a competent community organizer, doing the best that could be done with the human materials available—no worse than ours. Unless the Church of the apostles and martyrs legitimately realized his vision of society, he was kidding himself about his organizing role.

Therefore we needn't expect *our* work to produce a solider community than the early Church. We'll expect the first response to be an intense congregationalism based on critical local issues. A network of local communities will form where a national issue like the draft strikes home locally and an ideological response has been hammered out to it.

The original Church unity wasn't inherited from the Twelve Apostles but *achieved* in local congregations through organically developed forms of liturgy and ministry. Only afterwards did unity come to be felt between Churches in different cities, partly as natural growth, partly as takeover by the Roman administrative setup. The original impulse of the organizer can fade out in a few generations. And once the picture of origins preserved in the memory of institutional forms gets clouded, only a book can revive it. The Bible sits in judgment on the Church.

(c) The urgency of affirming community

There won't ever be an ideal State; there aren't even ideal principles for it. As soon as we've introduced one reform for justice we'll want to introduce another, until everything in the State denying true community has been disassembled. But we're willing to leave the State alone whenever any plausible change will likely be for the worse. In some countries we'd support a left-wing military dictator with a popular base, as the best available guarantee of stability and hopeful change. In a country fighting a colonial power we might put up with considerable restrictions on personal liberty, to assure the higher value of cultural survival—even though it's still only provisional too.

When an area has been deforested, a sequence of transitional shrubs and trees springs up, preparing the way for the climax forest, the natural cover. The Church is the sole natural climax canopy of human ecology: of course that doesn't prove it'll actually grow up everywhere someday. We can't acquiesce in compromise with the institutional Church as we do with the State. The definition of the Church is a zone overlapping the State where no compromise is necessary. One State is enough. The Saints didn't go to all that trouble just to make a little tyranny inside the big one. If somebody has found an area inside the Church where compromise seems necessary, it's really a part of the State which is calling itself Church illegitimately. My style may be to work inside a faulty traditional

Church for reform, or to cooperate with people who for good reasons can't hear the name of Jesus. But whatever I change or don't change, I'll be doing the thing that in my best judgment means actually affirming true community. Also of course I'll remember that the situation may change, or my judgment improve, so that I'm pushed into affirming community some other way.

Circumstances may prevent a man from realizing that he's doing this. But then, however formally correct his affirmation of community, it's not done in the full light of understanding and is liable to corruption. There's some lack of clarity or honesty in the program of an incognito secular Church which prevents me from speaking out my understanding of what I'm doing. If the Church is good enough for us, it's good enough for the people we're cooperating with. Other people aren't all that more stupid than I to be treated like kids forever. The whole point of Jesus' work is his openness; the only Messianic secret he holds back is that he *isn't* the Messiah.

If we can imagine Gandhi, Francis, King even more perceptive or committed, they would have been even more effective. We needn't choose between mass organization and intensive work with a small group. The deeper the personal relations in the group, the better based the mass organization. The Church is a natural outcome of the Twelve Apostles—both in their virtues and in their faults.

Church history since Constantine has been the rise and decline of an Establishment—the infiltration of the Church by the State. In America the decline has taken the form of segregation and denominationalism, which in capsule form illustrate a worldwide failure to deal with the crisis of violence. In recompense there has risen up in America a secular movement for peace and liberation, which is the bearer of the Spirit for our time—but stands in need of the explicit ideology of the Church. The form which cooperation of Christians has taken in the Movement is the key to renewal and reunion of the Churches; it's to begin as nascent local congregations, which then develop organs of cooperation as a nationwide movement. This renewed ecumenical peace and liberation community is a nucleus which potentially can melt the denominations together from below—that is, become the real Church here. America (as she claims) has a potential Messianic role, providentially prepared for by the missionary movement of the last century and the imperialism of this one. It could provide the shape of a restored worldwide peace Church, capable for the first time of entering into dialogue with Buddhism or other religions of nonviolence, and creating a planetary zone of resistance and reconciliation transcending the demonic State.

2. The breakdown of the Church Establishment

(a) The takeover of the historic Church

Nothing else in history quite prepares us for what has happened since the time of Jesus: the takeover of the Church which bears his name by a series of national and international Establishments. The bankruptcy of this development in America today is certified when *the Churches are revealed as helpless or compromised before every symptom in the crisis of violence.*

The environment. It's been outdoorsmen like Sierra Club members who've led the fight for national parks; doctors and scientists who've pressed for action on air and water pollution.

Radioactivity. The American Churches couldn't produce any consensus that the atom-bombing of Japan was *wrong.* The Churches haven't come up with any program to cut down on testing— much less on the whole war-machine it's part of.

Population planning. The Roman Church continues to man the ideological barricades here; but no Church makes it an effective item of spirituality to leave the earth less cluttered than we found it.

Neo-colonialism. The Churches, which claimed to be the nation's conscience, have contributed less to the anti-war movement than any group except the labor unions. The impregnable position of the military chaplains has riveted anti-communism tighter onto the Churches than onto any other segment of the educated community.

Racism. The Churches have talked big, even appropriated money, but done little. Where enlightened communities have made the token step of school integration, no means exists by which congregations could be bussed around to integrate Sunday morning. In unenlightened communities, the Churches are the command bunkers of segregation.

The tradition. Among clergy and educated laymen, understanding of the Bible and biblical languages has been going down —both absolutely, and much more so relative to the progress of scholarship. At the same time, old forms of language, liturgy, music (even when of obvious symbolic or aesthetic value) are being found irrelevant and tacitly dropped.

The Establishment, infiltrating the Church apparatus from above, has controlled the clergy, liturgy, teaching materials, action programs. As the pews were drained of the dissatisfied, the takeover was accepted by default. The structure of Massachusetts Congregationalism would have been the ideal way to start off a Christian society—if only it hadn't been devoted to exploitation. America would be a different place if Rhode Island or Philadelphia had set the tone instead.

So far as the ostensible Church shares in the character of the State, it falls in the same problematical category. To the extent that it's a scene of power and coercion—with endowments to wield, positions to fill, strings to pull, compromises to maintain—we can't fully understand it. As was the case with the university, the Church won such success that it presented the State with both the threat of a different principle, and the opportunity of a ready-made institution to be taken over. The only resistance has come from individuals.

People who think in categories derived from generalization are all at sea in dealing with the church. Dogmatists of the inside (Church historians) treat everything that has *called* itself Christianity as if it were an intelligible self-contained whole continuous with the New Testament. Dogmatists of the outside (anti-clericals, Marxists) accept the category "Church History" by turning it upside down. But distinctions can be made. In Europe, Russia, Latin America, the takeover of the Church has the form of an Established Church subordinate to the State. In Asia and Africa it has the form of a missionary colonialism. In the United States it has the twin forms of *denominationalism* (from European immigration) and *segregation* (an indigenous colonialism): our history has made us into a model of the worldwide problem.

(b) The fall of the Church under Constantine

The martyrs who resisted the Imperial cult—Ignatius, Polycarp, Justin, and the rest—now have *their* cult, celebrated for millennia: a link with the apostolic Church and Jesus. Unseen realities were still accessible to that Church, hovering in the clouds like the four Beasts in the mosaic of Santa Pudenziana. But it was operating out of instinct, not knowledge. It kept up its identification with the poor—but increasingly as objects of charity rather than as organizational base. It correctly understood the soldier's oath as sacrifice to the Genius of the Emperor—but didn't see violence or power as a central problem. Its quick submission to Establishment after the conversion of Constantine shows that inner defenses had broken down. The persecutions undermined the Church of Jesus in an unforeseen way, by making it forget that success was the big danger.

In its urban ghetto, moving towards neo-Platonic or Oriental dualism, it lost the Hebrew feeling for the natural order, and so couldn't deal with the myth of the end of the world. It lost also Paul's dialectic and Jesus' paradoxes; it no longer saw man as ambiguous. In its simple-minded perfectionism, it watered down its principles far enough so that hopefully they could be obeyed to the letter. The continuance of sin inside itself remained a serious problem to it.

Being in the right led the Church into the ultimate mistake of incaution. It never imagined the State would listen to it—much less be controlled by one of its own number. But Constantine, a uniquely fortunate military usurper, judged correctly that its symbols had won hearts and minds; it was a suitable tool of empire. What had been founded as counter-Establishment—reproducing the prevailing organization with opposite principle—was taken up, through its own merits, as the heart of Establishment.

It's easy to suggest that the rulers of the Church, while welcoming Constantine's adherence, should have urged his baptism more strongly and stood against his crimes. It's easy to see why they didn't. After the great persecutions of Diocletian, Constantine's victory was the providential release they'd been hoping for. Their lack of historical viewpoint made it easier for them to forget the Church of the martyrs, to misread the Gospels or leave them unread.

We interpreted the Fall of Man as the birth of conscious violence in the city-state—which still produced the splendors of Greek culture and Hebrew literature. We may look at the Establishment of the Church as a second fall—which still, as a by-product, generated European civilization. But history builds all crimes and errors along with the good into an intelligible pattern. The ecclesiastical jungle surrounds a secret fountain of youth; people keep getting the point concealed with such loving care.

The providential item in the fall of the Church was acquiring access to the top of society. Church historians, impressed like the rest of us with money and power, get so excited by this that they conclude Establishment was simply the right thing. We've seen too many prisons built with stones of law, brothels with bricks of religion, just to jump on the bandwagon. Was the fall necessary for the civilization? We don't have to decide. Our cue is simply to affirm the merits of the past while trying to avoid its errors—and never give up on the effort to separate them.

(c) The medieval Establishment

The medieval Church is the blurred mirror where we see the departing Teutonic and Celtic Gods—our own paganism. Europe is filled with holy places and things: the Ruthwell Rood with its Old English verse, the white sands of Iona, the battlemented cathedral of Prague, the sweetness of Bede's *History*, stones soaked with centuries of plainsong, of damp, of colored lights; Christmas and Easter and St. John's Eve and Halloween. At the English Reformation the processions became black-and-white, but the sacred language took on a new depth. The European parish behind us there, through its magic isolation, achieved an unparalleled union of peasant society into a whole culture.

But the compromises of the Church with the State kept going

further—beginning with Augustine's theory of the just war. And as the Church spread further into Europe, and the collaboration of Pope and Emperor was ever more presupposed, its God moved closer to the tribal Yahweh. The parts of the Hebrew Bible untouched with the spirit of prophecy—the coronation of Solomon, the wars of Joshùa—became more and more congenial. This re-Semitizing of medieval Christianity was strengthened by controversy with Islam, which as usual drove both parties into the same camp. The Crusades are a reflex of the *jihad,* a sacred war—and the Inquisition is their appropriate interior.

Again, contemporary with all this was the Francis who went to Church one day, heard the Gospel and applied it to himself. We don't look for him to have opposed Papal supremacy or the Crusades. But neither would we have looked for him to affirm the things he did: his happy coexistence with the created order, the realism in which he accepted the impress of the Cross, the fidelity of his identification with the poor.

(d) The two phases of the Reformation

Francis subverted the Establishment without either of them recognizing it. But Luther in his *Tractate* on Christian liberty broke halfway through the dead hand of the Establishment to radical personal liberation. We all know how he discovered that the Church is always liable to corruption and in need of reformation—identifying his own situation under Catholic legalism with Paul's situation under Pharisaic legalism. He represents a permanent principle of renewal which may have to be repeated until the end of time.

But Luther couldn't break through to radical *social* liberation. Like his contemporaries, he didn't read history with enough sympathy to see that primitive Christianity had been a counter-Establishment to the State. He was as dependent on entrenched aristocracy as his opponents; his condemnation of the Peasants' Revolt is a crusade, not a just war. He could get as far back as Paul, but not to Jesus.

At the same time as Luther's successful but partial renewal inside the Establishment, there was an arrested but radical reformation outside, in the sects. Protestant radicalism today is best represented by a distinguished anomaly of somewhat later origin, the Religious Society of Friends. It's bobbed up from proletarian George Fox to the Philadelphia aristocracy, keeping its primitive principles intact. The sects saw what Luther had overlooked, that by the Gospel the poor were designated as bearers of the future—a truth most clearly grasped in our own time by Marxists and nationalists.

The official Reformation of the Churches, new and old, involved a deeper surrender to the new States. The sectarian Reformation, potentially more thoroughgoing, was abortive and fragmented—as shown by its break with Catholic tradition, its weakness in effective concern for all society, its splintering. The Quakers lost sight of the primitive sacraments in a petrified liturgy, and dropped them. They've also lost Fox's spirit of active mission for his vision of the community of love. But precisely by not having to compete as one denomination among others, they were liberated to affirm the true form of community—a little out of the mainstream. Their vocation was *for our own decades:* to preserve intact certain essential truths until they could serve as the principles of renewal in the traditional Churches.

(e) The colonial missionary movement and segregation

A map of the nineteenth-century missionary Churches has the same colors as the map of colonialism. The missionaries operated inside a paternalistic framework which for them was unbreakable. Lanternari has shown that a forerunner of anti-colonialism is the evolution of missionary work into indigenous syncretistic Churches with local Messiahs, which in turn become the seedbed of revolution.

Colonized people overseas have grasped the principle of making decisions about their own future; rejecting the imperialist colonialism of Britain, the Low Countries, Spain; the cultural colonialism of France; the political colonialism of Russia; and now the economic colonialism of America. The missionary effort was an apparently inseparable mixture of religious imperialism and the Gospel; but nationalism is effecting the separation. The fault of the new Churches from now on won't be subservience; their divisions will cut across the Great Schism and the Reformation. The Churches of America and Europe have exhausted what they had to say to the Third World. If anybody, it's the new Churches which have something to teach us about the possibilities of man's existence on his soil.

We've seen the American black community as colonial enclave; its religious evolution follows the overseas pattern. Mostly the blacks are in their own denominations. Even in denominations theoretically integrated, the past year has seen the emergence of black caucuses—as in every other integrated group. "Black Christianity," like Black Islam, contains mythical elements. The dogma of a black Jesus, even if conjectural ethnography, affirms powerfully the historic identification of Jesus with the poor.

(f) Denominationalism as the heart of breakdown

Although the role of the black as former slave is unique, the melting pot in general is coming unstuck. Thus the working-class emigrants from eastern Europe in our central states are drawing back into their ethnic shell before the threat of black social mobility up towards them. Their splintered Orthodox Churches (with a largely sociological function) have never moved towards union with American Protestantism.

Emigration has made denominationalism in the U.S. a microcosm of world Christianity; except that (as Richard Niebuhr observed) European Churches became sects in America, and the sects became Churches. Middle-class immigrants from the Established Churches settled where they landed and became sectarian enclaves. The frontier was composed of sectarian fugitives both from Europe and the urban east coast; and it deposited an Established Church behind it, as the lip of the mollusk secretes the shell. The new frontier Churches were defenseless against Establishment, selecting its least attractive aspects. The European State Churches here gained more: legal disestablishment allowed them to keep traditional symbols, while radical Reformation insights became available to individuals.

The comparability of middle-class denominations had two results: it finally discredited the Constantinian Establishment; it allowed catholic and radical elements (catalyzed by a secular movement) to approach synthesis. As official bodies, the Establishment denominations can admit only a limited guilt for the crisis of violence—which comes out as a genteel cry for inner renewal and outer reunion. But the cry is hollow while their Establishment status forbids renewal on the issue of the actual exploitation, and reunion on the basis of such a renewal.

The suburban Churches can't bear the historic perfection of Gregorian chant, Latin, Lutheran chorales, Cranmer's English; and leap to the conclusion that *these* things are dividing them. So they drop those archaic monuments in favor of faddish improvisations, which reflect neither permanent meanings nor the current crisis. At the same time convictions—even among Catholics—about old theories of ministry, traditional forms of Church order, are melting into nothing. Actually what separates the middle-class denominations isn't what they once disagreed about, but the immobile meaningless thing they now *agree* on: the expensive staff which maintains white-elephant Churches, occupies ever-expanding headquarters, administers ambiguous charities, connives at war and exploitation, in general perpetuates itself.

As substantive issues evaporate, the respectable denominations are driven to find a formula of reunion—for the sake of administrative efficiency and public image. The Consultation on Church Union (COCU) is engineered by a club of graduates from the same seminaries, where acceptable Uncle Tom wings of Negro denominations are given token place. This top-level reunion is discovered to be a safe liberal issue, and everybody is told not to rock the boat. If consummated, it will simply widen the gap between the middle-class Churches and the poor black and poor white Churches. But accidentally it's let slip a secret; change is no longer unthinkable.

(g) The cry for radical renewal

The pressure of guilt in the face of unacknowledged crisis is polarizing the middle-class denominations. Conservatives keep getting shoved further into the Establishment bag. People who hear the cry for renewal and justice find their true allies among their counterparts in other denominations rather than in the underground part of their own, and are extruded into makeshift radical groupings. The same thing is happening in every other sector of American society—the university, the professions, young people, housewives. Out of the prophetic tradition preserved in fossilized institutions, the crisis of violence has generated a radical movement for justice and liberation.

More and more groups are being squeezed out from a narrowing consensus into subject status. The lot of the blacks has worsened both relatively and absolutely; the Latin American ghetto of New York has grown up since World War II, others have deteriorated. Young people unwilling to start up the affluence ladder can't find any middle ground, but are forced into hippie dropoutism. Critics or dissidents in one area must spread into other areas until their alienation is complete. The only solution is then to affirm that *they* are the America they want to stand for—the revolutionary posture.

To purge the guilt of suburban Churches, clergy are encouraged to invent radical new ministries—with failure built in to satisfy the conservatives. The clergy must cut themselves off from their Church base to win credibility among their new constituents. Then they're drained by service, they lose contact with the liturgy, and they never had been given the insight into the Bible to find something called God when men failed them. The system extrudes these irritants by getting them to discredit themselves. No hand is stretched out to help them when they end up casualties. It is this casualty list that must be built into a community.

As middle-class Christians become radicalized, their friendships sink through the levels of society to the dispossessed: blacks, students, deviates, draft-resisters, hippies. A radically ecumenical Church of intellectuals and the proletariat is emerging which sees the Establishment as colonial police power. As Asia and Africa pick up Western technology, America is being colonialized. So far as the Establishment Church loses its claim to be called *any* kind of Christianity, the religious scene here becomes identical with that in the Third World: a minority persecuted Church in coalition with revolutionaries.

3. The secular Peace and Liberation Movement

(a) The American movement of the sixties

Dissent and resistance today aren't a temporary phase in a single generation, but a response across all age-groups to the actual rhythm of events. Hiroshima came to Ben Spock as a mature professional; to men of my generation by the act of our comrades in arms; to my students in the monthly air-raid drill of their childhood, crouched under their little desks. Simultaneously for us all, the non-employment of nuclear devices in Viet Nam crystallized the meaning of Hiroshima—and of exploitation at home. As each of us surfaces from those underground years of puzzled alienation, we see others on the same path. While we correct each other's inadequacies, each rests on the inner strength of having made his own discoveries. We've become a movement.

The indigenous base of any revolution is the main block of the people being pushed around. Draft-eligible males are a semi-permanent exploited group. Tom Hayden, a founder of Students for a Democratic Society, also acts as ambassador at large of the shadow government to revolutions overseas. Some of us are trying to politicize the white hippie ghetto. In the Poor People's Campaign, as in the California Peace and Freedom Party, a strong push is being made to include American Indians and Latin Americans in a black-and-brown caucus—along with just plain poor whites. After all this has been said, the base of any radical change here will still be the black community.

The American movement became self-conscious in the Selma march under the leadership—never unquestioned—of Martin Luther King. Neither there nor in the anti-war movement did he quite hit on the creative risky step which would have put him in full control like Gandhi. But his assassination (April 4, 1968) marks a new phase. I asked one of my students what he found at Selma: "The primitive Church." The integrated fellowship of those days wasn't a temporary tactic leading up to something else; it was the very thing we were intending to affirm, a moment in the freedom song of the human spirit.

Soon after Selma in 1965, the consciences aroused there took on the burden of opposition to the war—the most moving episode of American history for a hundred years. Its greatest effectiveness lay at the points of maximum commitment and risk. The individual focus was personal non-cooperation with the draft resistance: first by young men like my friend Malcolm Dundas; then by their supporters like Robert McAfee Brown and William Sloane Coffin, those with the Berrigans who purified the draft board files by blood and fire, those who with Joan Baez were shipped off to Santa Rita Rehabilitation Center. The collective focus culminated in the confrontation at the Pentagon (October 21, 1967). In the face of this tremendous moral effort, Lyndon Johnson was forced to try and salvage things by refusing renomination and ending the bombing of Hanoi (March 30, 1968). The protest at Chicago in August of 1968 didn't have anything new to teach Americans about the war —only about themselves.

(b) The ideology of the Movement

So far as it's dealing with causes and not just symptoms, the Movement claims to be *building a new society in America*. Old institutions are being dismantled in the fundamental way of subtracting actual men and women from them, and building them into new institutions of parallel function and different structure. On a broad front ranging from anarchism to humanism to revolutionary socialism, the Movement is doing its best to affirm the true form of community.

Richard Shaull, in an unpublished paper, has drawn out the case for assent to revolution at whatever violence-level proves necessary. He assumes that conditions of living have changed through generations; that an ever-increasing "rationalization of economics" opens before us; that we're set on a one-way "desacralization" of nature and of old social patterns; that we're permanently committed to the new sensibility of the McLuhan era. He sees the thing wrong with existing institutions to be not so much their violence (as I do) but simply their being *old*. Since we must come to terms with innovation, whatever assists the breakdown of the old bears its legitimacy on its face.

I see certain old forests, old books, old men, as intrinsically sacred. Much of what is called "rationalizing economics" seems actually to be flying in the face of inescapable ecological laws. Our psyche or community isn't endlessly plastic, and instant information does them violence. The very justice and success of revolution in Russia and America has made them so big a threat to the planet. The ambiguity of history indicates that it's impossible and unwise to set up unified plans for national or global economics; rather, we must demand decentralized planning, coordinate resistance against usurpations.

Some revolutionaries see the changeover from a peasant to an industrial economy in Russia and China as a precedent for the rest of Asia, Africa, Latin America. But Russia and China are much bigger than the Third World countries, and were never colonialized. Even less do those revolutions offer a plausible precedent for what might happen in America, since they bear little resemblance to the British, French, or American Revolutions, or our Civil War.

This debate about violence belongs inside the Movement, where it's resolved into an internal discussion between Christianity and Marxism—on a more fundamental level than the academic debate begun by Garaudy. The most articulate spokesmen for nonviolence in the Movement, like Barbara Deming, don't come at it from a specifically Christian viewpoint. But, as they're the first to admit, they stand in the direct tradition of Gandhi and Muste. Their saint is the Quaker confessor in flames, Norman Morrison; we're touched to see his portrait on a postage stamp from Hanoi. The natural role of Christians in the Movement is to speak for nonviolence: finding an alternative to joining the Viet Cong or Black Panthers.

The Marxist wing of the Movement has been strongly modified toward people's revolution. Its writers are Régis Debray and Frantz Fanon, self-conscious ideologists of liberation. Its hero is Ernesto Che Guevara, murdered in Bolivia. The two wings can close ranks on Dietrich Bonhoeffer and Camillo Torres, ministers of Christ who chose the underground.

The current focus of the Movement is less on ideology than on jobs to be done; but a man who's grown gray in its service is likely to be holding on by virtue of some clear commitment as a Catholic, a Quaker, a Communist. As they work for specific goals by coalition with groups of differing ideology, the nonviolent wield a disproportionate influence, since nonviolence can always be agreed on by a coalition at least as tactics. Establishment pacifists shy away from coalition as compromising the purity of their witness. But radical pacifists realize no witness is required in the pure society of their fellows, and are only seen in the councils of the violent.

(c) The Peace Movement as bearer of the Spirit

The situation of the Peace Movement channeled it into nonviolent protest and resistance. It could only associate itself with the urban black rebellion as sympathetic outsiders, "concerned honkies." Overwhelming police force has pushed even militant blacks into advocating violence only for self-defense.

The Movement runs parallel to the Galilean Resistance. Both echo the prophetic cry for justice and self-determination. In their political mood each has looked for a military liberator Messiah: a John of Gischala, fortifying the Jerusalem ghetto against the Roman armies, an Eldridge Cleaver. But both, in spite of dark expectations, are led by preponderance of Establishment power into symbolic nonviolent resistance. And both have a non-political mood in which they see the true Liberated Zone as precisely the act of loving resistance, where the dissenting community is cast in a revised Messianic role. Somebody has said that Marxism with its cry for justice and its secular eschatology is a Christian heresy. We may say that *the Peace and Liberation Movement is a Christian orthodoxy.*

Of course *it* can't say so. The divine language of the New Testament has been pre-empted by an Establishment Church and is unavailable. And it shouldn't say so. The Messiah, incognito to himself, must be recognized by the faithful community.

As soon as we locate the objective marks of the early Church —its poverty, comradeship, increase under persecution, ideals of integrity—we see they're things not merely illustrated by the Movement, but *best* illustrated by it in our time. People once found

M

elements of Christianity in the trade-union movement. Looking back we now see, by its very success, how far it was the self-assertion of a single class. In the current Movement, the goals are more far-reaching, the means necessarily more risky, the coalition more extensive. Like the early Church, it builds on the disenfranchised; it's oriented toward specific issues of personal liberation; it emphasizes commitment and local autonomy. Its traveling community organizers have to win the confidence of local groups honestly—by holding themselves up to an even higher standard. As we try to define its historic role, we're bound to say: *The Peace and Liberation Movement is the bearer of the Spirit to our age.*

That's not to say the Movement will remain so forever. It fell into that historic role almost without ideology, under the push of circumstance. Another turn of events could modify its nonviolence which so strikingly commends the Gospel, but which it adopted tactically. The Church has to seize the hour and call the new thing by its right name, or it will lose the hour.

(d) The Church as servant of the Movement

If an ideology can show that history isn't dead but lives on in us, we have grounds to feel that we shan't die either, but live on in the future. There was an independent discovery of Western truths in the Buddhist tradition. On the strength of it we hold out our hands to our alleged enemies as to brothers. But even in Berkeley, Buddhism is a pretty exotic import. If ever the Church is to discover whether Gautama is a mask of the Christ or something else, we'll first have to regroup around the primitive Church.

The Movement correctly sees Christians as capable of being shamed, perhaps converted. If someday outsiders no longer note the Church's hypocrisy, it'll mean that they no longer see a contrast between practice and message—the message will have become inaudible. The Movement can't cover up the fact that (due in large part to its influence) there's growing up, cutting across all denominational lines, a Church inside the Church which bears a resemblance to the Movement and to her own founder. Remembering that out of Jefferson and Adams came the foreign policy of Lyndon Johnson, that out of Marxism came Stalin, that out of Jesus came the Renaissance popes and Francis Cardinal Spellman, we can't be too careful about sending a community into the future with the right marching orders.

This is one planet, one race of men. Everything bears in itself the mark of a single origin. Our asymmetric molecules are all right-handed, as they came out in the first crystallization of life; all quadrupeds have the same skeletal structure. A philosopher can only be described as a man doing in his own time what Socrates did in his. And so a man of reconciliation can only be described as one doing in his time what Jesus did in his. The Church of Jesus is the unique permanent carrier of love.

The human race can only become the unity which in principle it is, if each solemnly takes off his old clothes, spattered with blood and dirt, and undertakes to go a new way. And the new way is to sit down and break bread together, each deferring to his neighbor. So the Church of Jesus is constituted by those two actions of washing and eating, with a form of words referring to his example. If there is only one trail up the mountain, and it's been clogged by briers and fallen trees and washouts, the only thing is for the Outing Club to go and open it up again.

4. A liberated Church in America

(a) The failure of renewal in the denominations

Up until now, renewal has been non-congregational: in peace fellowships; groups for racial justice, ecumenical study, liturgical experiment; ministries to the disenfranchised—teen-agers, students, prostitutes, the colored, the unemployed, migrants, immigrants. The obstacle to renewed congregations is denominational jealousy. The Churches, slipping back from their prosperity in the Eisenhower years, have a long nose for competition. While they cling to old forms of liturgy and government with determination and without conviction, they decree a noninstitutional structure for the special ministries which they send out on their short tethers.

A campus theologian whom I deeply respect urged me to go on working inside the denominations and existing ecumenical structures as long as I conscientiously could. I asked him what he would recommend, beyond the transitory forms of campus Christianity, if students at his university should become interested in the Gospel. He recommended campus Christianity *because* it was transitory. He couldn't for their sakes wish them in his denomination, or its competitors. But in a long-term revolution we *must* have institutions that define our permanent commitment. Our duty isn't sentimental adherence to the old for as long as possible, but helping some institution to emerge that represents our true feelings, that we can recommend without apology.

What the denominational office does is on balance an obstacle to renewal.

(1) *Faith and morals.* Most official statements are not a guide or support but something we have to explain away. Rome does better than most on social issues, worse than most on personal ones. The National Council of Churches comes at us with less canonical authority than our denomination, less moral authority than our own hearts.

(2) *Literature.* The denominationally sponsored liturgy, hymnal, educational materials, devotional manuals, catechism, calendar of saints, rule of discipline, don't say any longer the things we need to have said. Each renewed community is putting together its own materials—in union with other groups elsewhere and not with the denomination.

(3) *Organization.* The denomination publishes a list of authorized congregations and clergy with whom we're supposed to agree, be in full "communion," cooperate on joint projects; others are at most recognized by some exception or charity. But now we find ourselves the best or only judge of our comrades—the people who share our commitments.

(4) *Clergy.* The theoretical control by the denominations duplicating seminary standards channels timid seminarians into conservatism, and sets up arbitrary hurdles for the liberated. Seminarians who are academically superior and psychologically independent go into teaching, the Peace Corps, non-parochial work.

(5) *Testimony.* We ask that anybody who calls himself our

moral leader should have resisted the war and what it stands for. Denominational leadership by its nature is incapable of taking this kind of risk. Now that the Gospel finally has come once again to mean standing over against the State, we must look elsewhere for leadership.

The hierarchies in practice have given up the traditional claims of their denominations as written into confessions or liturgy. They simply control existing bodies of people which represent money and influence. The labels which tag those institutions mean as little to members as to leaders. The community organizer is glad to operate through middle-class institutions which have lost their soul, holding in his hands that key to their guilt. But we who're persuaded that the charter of the Church defines where *we* stand can't manipulate it from the outside. If the Church or some bit of it makes a claim for herself, we have to consider it seriously and then accept or reject it; we can't pretend to ignore it.

The last recourse of the denominations to hold our loyalty is to confess that they're in transition; we must be patient until they decide what they are. But they've been doing this for too long now. Nobody can be satisfied forever with an institution which proclaims his principles in theory but ignores them in practice, tolerates his private adherence to them, and prevents him from working them out in community.

The Churches, like the other institutions of our unified society, evolved into a shape where they were vulnerable to demonic invasion. The situation is a *responsibility vacuum.* No denomination today takes seriously the claim which all once made, to represent the true form of the Church. Therefore none can speak responsibly, either here or in relaying the pronouncements of an overseas headquarters. But neither have they found a way to delegate responsibility to the National Council of Churches or anything else. It's this vacuum, swept and garnished, that the demons have moved into. *The crisis of violence concentrated in this war,* which has shown up so many other institutions of our society, *has also radically discredited the denominations of American Christianity and their top-level ecumenism.*

(b) Saying Yes and No to the denominations

If Church history did no more than reflect political history, we should still expect a major reorientation of the Church scene in response to the crisis of violence. And what if it's the Church that goes *farthest* in defining an age's meaning, for better or worse? The surprise God still has up his sleeve may be an intensification of its possibilities. Nothing in principle forbids new modes of ecumenism, styles of sanctity, levels of dialogue with other ideologies. We can also imagine an Establishment Church even more deeply identified with a war machine than before.

Many outsiders are ready to take a renewed Christianity as seriously as Christians are willing to take it. They accept Marxism wherever it's useful. We claim that Marxism is a fragmentary, secularized Christianity. We dare point to the Gospel as a symbolism of hope, free from utopian illusions, which recognizes that every movement for truth—beginning with itself—can be corrupted into a bearer of evil.

But first the Church crisis has to be resolved in its twin forms of Establishment takeover and denominationalism—heresy and schism. The situation would be different if America had a monolithic Established Church, whether "Catholic" or "Protestant." But the fragmentation of American Christianity is one of the facts in which history has embodied our hope. We must learn to be dialectical, to say both Yes and No to the Church structures we've actually got.

Saying Yes to the Churches. The formal claim of each denomination to be the true descendant of primitive Christianity for our time, however little believed, still serves a useful purpose for it. Because if we drop denominational principles, we're put in the position of seeming to drop primitive Christianity also. We must say Yes to the thing it professes while pointing out the inconsistencies in its profession.

We must also say Yes to their monopoly on an ecclesiastical Establishment: we don't want any part of it. We must resist the temptation to set up a counter-Establishment outside; that would mean that they had converted us. Rather we must set up a counter-Establishment *inside*.

Above all we must say Yes to the things we've gotten from the existing Church. We're its sons; from its Bible, its prayer book, its baccalaureates, we learned the principles by which it could be judged and renewed.

The strength of reform sentiment in the Church comes from academic and professional middle-class homes. Likewise for the Movement—it's a secularized version of the cry for Church reform. Reconciliation means not giving up on people and groups—including the Establishment. We built everything into the Liberated Zone that will let itself be built.

It's as hard staying in touch with the past as with a spaceship or a star. The velocity of light surprises us; so short a distance in time corresponds to so great a distance in space. The hypocrisy and compromise of the Church Establishment are noisy channels through which the saints of the past communicate necessary information to us.

There's a masochist in each of us, hoping the Establishment will come down on us like a ton of bricks, so we can prove how obnoxious it is. We all have programmed into us a track for failure. We should be encouraged to bypass it; the cosmos has arranged plenty of routes for failure without our picking one out for ourselves.

Saying No to the Churches. The denominations measure their success by budgets and statistics, sacraments of an affluent society. We must take those security-blankets away from them, while affirming that we're carrying out the real goals for which they once came into being. We may make it easy for creative groupings inside them to shift allegiance—but put the burden of proof on them to show that they stand for something important enough to warrant continuance.

The Establishment surely must be asking something of every person which he has the power to refuse. Of young men it asks their bodies. Of the middle class it asks taxes, and we should go on thinking about imaginative schemes for tax-refusal. But of everybody the Establishment expects *assent*, as expressed by adherence to symbolic institutions. Johnson felt it important to attend Church, even at some risk of hearing the truth. The Churches are heaped with draft-exemptions, tax-exemptions, social security benefits, military chaplaincies. The acquiescence of Churches in the war kept dissent fragmented, persuaded the Administration it could weather the storm. Refusal of this assent by Church people would powerfully shake the Establishment's self-esteem.

I don't propose resignation from the Church or from the reality behind the denominations, but resignation from the Establishment. We look for the resignation of people in Government, the military, draft boards, defense industries. But we're no less involved in the Establishment than they are. The Churches are no purer, benefit just as much. These people are waiting for us as their self-proclaimed moral leaders to set the example.

The Church isn't threatened by people dropping into secularism or some other denomination; this affirms the denominational principle all over again. But it would be threatened by people dropping out into ecumenism—by the possibility of reunion on radical principles. As the cry for top-level reunion grows louder, the conservative lay lawyers prolong our opportunity by blocking even those paper schemes. We must use our time to *pre-empt the claim that Church reunion has taken place in the Peace and Liberation Movement.*

Those who've rejected the corruption of the Churches are afraid it will happen all over again if reunion comes. Of course it will. It will begin weakly in a radical reunion; it will be built in from the beginning in a top-level reunion. But if we're convinced that reunion is in the cards, we should opt for the best kind we can get. We have the chance of forestalling corruption just so far as we can work in the principles of nonexploitation and participatory democracy.

The dilemma about saying Yes and No to the Establishment is resolved when we see that the Establishment isn't the key to the problem. Our cue is to find the creative thing to do in face of the critical need, and let the Establishment decide whether this is subversion or renewal. We can go on recognizing as our brothers whoever affirms what we affirm, whether they're continuing Catholic priests or Quakers. We recognize our sister liberated congregations, Churches, fellowships, without formal standards of recognition. The standards will only be needed when trust starts to evaporate.

Likewise we're not to make up our minds in advance that some large conservative Establishment Church is going to be left in schism outside. We'll try to liberate people and groups to work constructively in her. We'll welcome flexibility of arrangements which to her will seem intolerably ambiguous. And we'll remember that *we're the part of her which has entered into effective reunion.* We still have a foot in the old camp. As we stand there, seeming to say Yes and No simultaneously to the Church, we're really calling its attention to more important things which it's been ignoring: the cry of suffering humanity, the call of the Spirit.

(c) The Movement as catalyst of Church renewal

Once again the Church has fallen into its regular apostasy: identifying itself with the errors of the society it was supposed to transform. The problem of the thirteenth century was success and ennui. An order of renewal inside the existing Church recaptured a spirituality of the poor on their land—at the expense of palliating deeper-seated corruptions. The problem of the sixteenth century was new wine in old wineskins: ever more inelastic solutions were being offered for new discoveries, geographical, intellectual, social. The resolution was a breakaway; even though the Reformers weren't careful enough to avoid divisions, and failed to grasp the historical Jesus.

The twentieth century combines these problems: ennui with the American way of life, the meaninglessness of denominationalism beside new social structures. And it adds to them an unparalleled crisis of violence. What conceivable renewal will do for this century?

There the reunion-spinners sit in the cobwebs of their ecumenical workshops, calling for a grass-roots base. I say that the Church has already found a sidewalk base. We're on the only possible ground if we can recognize as our own some movement which is already capturing the best spirits in the Churches; if we give it its true name, guide it on the path it's started to walk, save it from the mistakes it would like to make. As soon as we say this, we realize that we know it; it's called, simply enough, the Movement. Because people have put the Kingdom and justice first, those things which once seemed to separate us have vanished. Nothing is wanting to reunion with our Christian brothers but our recognition of it.

We haven't got a mission to call the Movement into a Church whose unity is prefabricated. If it moves towards the Church, it will indeed find a potentially unifying ideology there. But it will find renewed Christianity as fragmented as itself—and along the same lines: student Christians and student radicals, black Christians and black radicals, pacifist or revolutionary Christians and pacifist or revolutionary radicals, God-is-dead Christians and secular radicals. Because the Movement and the Church are two fountains from a single pipe; their overlapping is the decisive thing which determines the form of our renewal.

Unlike Hitler's Germany, our best people aren't emigrating but staying on. The Resistance—including what's been called the Christian Resistance—won't disband after the Viet Nam war until the people in prison have received amnesty; until arrangements are made for the resisters to go and do reparation for their country in Viet Nam (and Laos and Thailand and Cambodia); until the defective heart of America has been replaced by a transplant. Staughton Lynd has said that the summer in Mississippi working on civil rights has expanded into a lifetime family vocation.

We'd said all along that reunion wouldn't be the work of men but of the Spirit; little did we know what we were letting ourselves in for! We've lost interest in the old stale chewing-gum debates as our self-affirmation crystallizes around the freedom to say, "We must obey God rather than men" (Acts 5:29). Up until now, apart from the trauma of the Civil War, we've been just playing at keeping house on this continent. Now the honeymoon is over. For the first time we can talk seriously about the Church in America.

We must put aside resentment at the complicity and cruelty of the Establishment, pushing through to the other side of our impotence. Because revolution is in the air, the Liberated Zone is at hand. Decisive novelties in history must pass over a high threshold of reserve. Their fuel is the hidden backlog of disgust and resolve in millions of individuals. But after so many false alarms and pseudo-Messiahs people are wary; they're waiting for the unmistakable trumpet of the Spirit.

The Vietnamese affirm that the forms of their new societies are hammered out through resistance to oppression. Every leader in Hanoi received his baptism in a French jail; the political structure of the National Liberation Front was formed in answer to *us*. And so we may say that Lyndon Johnson was the prime organizer of the liberated Church in America.

The Movement is the midwife of renewal. All along it's been the Church outside the Church, doing what Jesus did, being what he was. As soon as we recognize it without reserve—bringing to it our own historical understanding—the Church will start moving into the depth and kind of unified renewal which was in the books for our time. The standards which show the failure of the denominations point to the emergence of the right thing somewhere else. What has been heralded as the death of God was actually the death of the Churches. *L'Église est morte. Vive l'Église!*

It's not the case that a little group of perfectionists in each denomination is being siphoned off to form a new sect, nor that a new alternative style of ecumenical ministry is being offered in each denomination. Separatism and tolerance are just two different ways of being put on the shelf. Our new principle of unity lies in the necessary jobs which the denominations by their Establishment status are precluded from doing.

Existing structures are on the right track if they can accept allegiance on a provisional basis from the gadflies on the rump of the sleepy animal. The clergy are under no call to give up their ministry, or anything else good and true which they (like other Christians) have received. Rather they'll say they're fulfilling those things. If the denomination wants to excommunicate or depose them, that's its business. It can hardly render them less effective than they are now. We'll continue to affirm the real values of our denomination—facets of the truth in Jesus—in the status of renewal and reunion. We can't rule out the possibility that living renewal

might thaw out frozen structures from beneath; that it might infil-
trate formal schemes of reunion struggling down from above and
give them actual content.

Church reform has always taken shape from the struggle to
deal with current crises. So renewal and reunion in America can
only come out of our struggle to deal with the crisis of violence,
where the Viet Nam war in its time has been central. But the best
of our Christian leaders are already fully engaged, fully united in
that struggle. Therefore renewal has already set in.

*At the right time of history, a liberated Church in America has
been born out of the Movement for peace and justice.*

5. The functions of a renewed Church

(a) The liberated Church as community

Renewal crystallizes a group of people around work on a particular concern, whether local or national. The community—which
we may call a local congregation—becomes our proper environment for various functions.

In our personal crises: getting into college, sex, draft-resist-
ance, getting married, getting a job, getting fired, divorce, bankruptcy, mental breakdown, dealing with kids, success, death of
parents, moving, sickness, retirement, dying. It surrounds us with
sympathetic persons who, for the moment, have a different crisis
from ours. It makes available to us jointly symbolic forms ("sacraments") which define for each crisis the shape of the nonviolent
revolution—the mind of Christ.

On our individual job. It provides a framework of action and
teaching where its members transform the neutral technique of
their professions into a sign of the new way. It shows that certain
professions—arms manufacture, the military, many police jobs,
many government jobs, most advertising—are impossible for the
honest man; and that all must be preserved from manipulation. It
defines new professions—community organization, overseas service—which will carry out its principles.

In education, service, action. It operates on behalf of its principles to educate the community outside, to provide medical or social

services which have slipped through the meshes of the Establishment, to affect politics, to dramatize injustice by direct action.

The community solidifies in two critical areas: the rural ghetto; and the city, where an urban ghetto and concerned intellectuals overlap. Typical rural ghettos are the South, California's migrant farmers, Indian reservations, the Spanish Southwest, poor white Appalachia. The leader of the poor, a Tijerina or Chavez, may spring direct from the soil. But in any case he must make alliance with the city—for warm bodies, money, organization, ideology, allies.

The black or Spanish urban ghettos have now mostly developed indigenous leadership. But they also need alliances, however tense, with the concerned white community to influence politics, for money, for solidarity in anti-war action. Such unity as the Peace Movement possesses comes from national organizations with autonomous urban branches. The apostolic Church was an urban movement; so was Marxism until it went guerrilla.

The organizer builds on an oppressed group, or on the psychic exploitation felt by its sympathizers. Students around the world have chosen exploited status. As the Church shares its origin with the university, it can look for joint liberation. In its nascent congregations, the way people work together determines the shape of renewal and the meaning of reunion.

(b) The forms of a liberated Church

Reunion presupposes the emergence of a common mind in various areas. This common mind is already taking shape through cooperation of Christians in the Movement.

Doctrine. Christian leaders in the Movement lack the liberal or sectarian features of American Christianity. The Movement's turning away from exploitation supports the teaching of Jesus more firmly than denominational creeds and disciplines do. Our return to Jesus rests on a thoroughly *historical* understanding of his role in a revolutionary situation. The Movement is the best place today to appreciate Hebrew social prophecy; the community organizer has a unique insight into Epistles and Acts.

The ministry. The old controversies about orders have been solved by unquestioning mutual recognition; the good faith of anybody ordained for a Christian community is taken for granted. Nobody would claim to be a Christian in the Peace Movement unless he really was; it brings no status or rewards. We learned this first from the politics of coalition; every overworked underpaid leader of an actual base of people represents them legitimately.

The denominational seminaries are discovering they've got nothing unique to teach, and so are merging—while still in theory preparing clergy for the denominations. This has produced an intolerable split of academic from personal convictions. For after full ecumenical training, students can't stay loyal to the denominations until decades from now the word comes down from on high that reunion has happened.

What's happening to the ministry could be termed either guerrilla subversion or normal growth inside the Establishment. It's still in missionary status—like the new Churches of Africa and Asia, before they won an indigenous ministry. (They still haven't reached the stage of indigenous theological seminaries with locally recruited professors.) In spite of these holdovers from colonialism, the new Churches could strain out from the traditional curriculum the things of local value—they're closer to the apostolic Church than their teachers. When young men go to an American seminary to serve in a radically reunited congregation, this will serve notice that denominationalism has become the foreign missionary body.

Spirituality. Nowhere else are secular people so willing as in the Movement to work with Christians as leaders or followers, to take our symbolic forms seriously. In the urgency of coalition effort the barriers to listening have fallen. *The Movement is the primary missionary field of the Church.*

The Movement has had a line of saints and martyrs in whose strength it does its work: Peter Maurin, A. J. Muste, Norman Morrison, Jonathan Daniels. The personal lives of its rank and file are in much disorder. They accept this as a revolutionary necessity, but still welcome concern. We chaplains to the Movement spend a lot of time in pastoral work with new twists: visiting courts and prisons, marriage counseling, activating dropouts, draft counseling.

Denominational weddings are going out even for Catholics. Even when the family breaks up, the generation gap has been bridged. The hippie kids who used to sneak out of Sunday school now sneak out of high school to join their elders at demonstrations and do their own mind-blowing thing. Some teen-age girls are important political figures with a bona fide constituency. You can hear seventeen-year-old kids lecturing gray-haired Quakers on nonviolent tactics.

The liturgy. The heart of the nascent groupings in the Movement is the Lord's Supper, celebrated any time but Sunday, anywhere but in Churches. Traditional differences in its understanding have evaporated through concelebration and freedom to improvise —within the definition of its meaning provided by the action context. On some occasions members of the Society of Friends, discovering new allies, have wished to join in the Eucharist.

Conversion. One feature of primitive Christianity has found an equivalent, but not yet renewal, on the contemporary scene: making a fresh start. The draft-card turn-in has exactly the format and meaning of the Baptist revival meeting: renouncing the world, the flesh, and the Devil; washing off the number of the Beast. Our theologians realize that infant baptism has become meaningless, and are moving toward a Baptist theory of adult initiation. The rebaptism of Reformation radicals had an unfortunate suggestion of perfectionism. *Conditional baptism* is indicated in the numerous cases where nothing definite can be said about the manner or intentions of infant baptism. We need a push to give proper symbolic form to the day-by-day dedication that already exists in the Movement.

(c) A new congregationalism

The form of renewal we're led to is what my student and colleague Dick York, in characteristic hippie style, calls a Free Church—but with unexpected overtones of the radical Reformation. Traditional Protestantism has been much concerned about maintaining local orthodoxy through higher structures. But we don't feel a synod or national organization will have *any* orthodoxy that doesn't percolate up from the bottom. What was the Reformation afraid of? —Deviation from an ideological and disciplinary scheme. But the only thing we have to fear is apostasy, finking out, which can't be predicted or hidden. Since the motive of renewal is a job of rebuilding to be done, the fears which produced the need for central organization are gone.

The older "community Churches" are similar in form to the nascent autonomous congregations, but different in substance. They're products of liberalism, aiming at maximum inclusiveness on the basis of minimum agreement, formed out of the denominations as a least common denominator. They're bound hand and foot to a geographic suburb, and haven't got any prophetic voice.

Since there's no intention of forming a new denomination, our current denominational ties (however illogical) deserve to be kept up on Alinsky's principle of despoiling the Egyptians. The Viet Cong use the supply-lines of the opposition, sending their kids to school overseas on government grants, picking up U.S. medical equipment on the Saigon docks. In our loving guerrilla tactics against the Establishment we do it the favor of intruding militants or hippies into diocesan conventions. We should put so much reality into our projects that the denominations, against their better judgment, will compete to support them.

If the liberated Church were inside the Establishment, it would be co-opted; if it were outside, it would be ignoring the claim of the denominations to represent the spirit of Jesus. It's a new shoot springing from the redwood stump. We need a sanctuary inside the Establishment where we're safe from both control and expulsion. We do this by plugging into the scene where the Church is conscious of guilt: guilt at not doing the ghetto job; at not telling the truth even as she sees it, let alone as it stands in the Gospel; at segregation and disunion. The middle-class silent fragmented Church is self-condemned. So whatever can claim legitimately to be a classless witnessing united Church has its hooks in the Establishment; it has proved its right to existence *aboveground*.

Nothing has been more important for liberation than the massive renewal inside the Roman Catholic Church—the only one being led from overseas. An outsider doesn't know which things its members can get away with and which they can't, but they do, which is all that counts. They've played some of the most creative risky roles in the Movement: Fr. James Groppi in the Milwaukee open-housing campaign; the Berrigan brothers, prisoners for Christ. The terms on which they can cooperate with us are our best check on getting too far away from base.

We put workers among alcoholics, ex-cons, grape-pickers— with the tacit presumption that our ecumenical representatives will do good social service but above all things not preach the Gospel. What will happen when the beneficiaries call our bluff and ask this detached clergyman to build them into a congregation?

In most areas of life sanctions limit our freedom. We're free not to go out and fight wars, but we may get jailed for it. We're free to study whatever we please, but we may not get a diploma or jobs for it. The Church is where we hold the future in our own hands. None of the rewards it offers are tickets to be turned in for goods and services somewhere else: money, a passport, a social security card, a draft card. The realm of the Church is the things which can be had simply by affirming them: self-fulfillment through life in community.

Any group of people that wants to form a Christian fellowship is able to; *there's no need to ask somebody else's permission.* They won't separate themselves from their brothers, inside or outside the Church, any more than they need to: rather they'll let others do the separating. The whole point of Christian fellowship is solidarity with those who disapprove of us. Whenever fellowship fails, as it may well, the failure lies in us and not in something else. But if we've tried honestly, it hasn't really failed.

The blasphemy in the Church Establishment is that the one liberated phase of society has been co-opted by the forms of the State. In fact the State stumbled accidentally on the true principle of Church unity: tolerance. Christians should make a radical claim to the freedom of association theoretically guaranteed by the State and practiced by the Movement. This unqualified freedom lies at the heart of our restricted political freedom. We can do what we please.

We don't reject existing Churches for being enmeshed in a meaningless denominationalism; we hold out something better, and

N

aren't offended if they don't accept it the first time. Englishmen touched by the Evangelical revival of the late eighteenth century couldn't stay permanently in Deist Tory parishes. They took over an old parish or built a new one, and preached the word of God as they heard it to new classes of people that were ready to listen. Only by that route did renewal make its way back to the old congregations.

Likewise, men touched by the Catholic liturgical revival of the past century and a quarter couldn't go on indefinitely being passive spectators of corrupt sacerdotal performances. They found a place where they could work out their new understanding—often among the new or old slums where Methodists or Evangelicals had paved the way. The renewal of our times presupposes everything valid in the earlier ones, but cuts far deeper. And it will take over the old Churches only along the same route.

Why should congregations ever again voluntarily submit to distant control by governing bodies, which in turn are tied to the policy of an exploitative State? At all times a double motion is required of us. We must gather ourselves apart sufficiently so that we can see for ourselves, and show to the world, what we are. After we've done that will be time enough to redisperse, and become once again the new leaven bubbling up through the vast soggy doughy mass. Our final push will be to find ways of working which carry out both motions at once.

(d) Speaking to the Church Establishment

In the 1830's and 40's the Churches overwhelmingly took up no stand on slavery at all. Today somebody who said that slavery *under that name* was the will of God would be called a heretic. If the Church is really the conscience of mankind, it would be nice for her to say what was needed when it was needed. The stridency of Abolitionism is said to have made Emancipation more difficult; I don't know that the Churches sitting on their hands made it any easier.

Our spiritual ancestors couldn't make up their minds until History had acted, pushed by men with actual convictions; then they saw which way the wind *had blown*. Not everybody criticizes them for this. The silence of Protestant Episcopal Bishops during the Civil War made it possible for the dioceses of North and South to be reunited afterwards, when most Protestant denominations split. What price was unity bought for? Slavery has now bloomed into a hundred flowers of discrimination and harassment. And once again, in the councils of the Church, unity (of those already inside) and gradualism are the overriding considerations.

Gradualism, as soon as you think about it, insults both the morals and the intelligence of the people you're trying to drag along. They aren't given credit for openness to the evidence which has convinced you. They must be bullied or cajoled a little bit every year, every decade.

Until recently, the Church Establishment recognized the right of a minority to have a special concern for nonviolence or justice —provided it stayed a minority. The minority professed to regard the majority as wrong but sincere. No dialogue was going on. Both sides assumed that some other issue—unity of the denomination— was more important. But the equilibrium will fall if the minority starts winning converts, or if it comes to decide that morality takes precedence over a united front.

Both things have happened. We don't ask the Establishment's permission to hold a higher private morality; we don't claim to be better, but to see more clearly. We don't say we agree with the Establishment on fundamentals; right now the fundamental thing is what we disagree on. But we won't pull out, because we can't let the Church of Jesus abdicate its function as bridge between his scattered communities and the world.

When somebody addresses himself in print to the President of the United States, we all know it's rhetoric with a different audience in mind. But our Church leaders can't have made the same paralyzing commitments as an American President, or gotten imprisoned in the same parallelogram of forces. They still remember how they first became servants of the Gospel—the only commitment they're bound to. Today they're faced with the chance that it may apply to them in a more detailed way than they thought possible.

Our religious leaders talk about existential concern. I turn to them and ask if we Americans in the sixties aren't men and women waked out of sleep with a choice we've got to make for ourselves, which no prior commitment can preempt. In these years we've seen growing up around us, inside the Churches and even more outside, but always under the authority of Jesus, groups where the demons of violence and exploitation have been exorcised. We can't pass the buck of deciding whether the philosophy of nuclear deterrence ends up in a world at peace—or else in a global poker game which hasn't got any breaking-up time, or breaks up with shooting irons.

No future age can be counted on for higher motivation than ours to do the necessary things. It's alleged that if we set up the right situation by force, the next generation will accept it with love. But our resentment will mold the attitudes of the next generation —which in any case can discover resentment for itself. The direct approach is the only approach there is. The only way to stop violence is to stop; love is the only way to make love.

If we see demons being cast out, it doesn't matter whose name it's done in; because it can only be done in the way of reconciliation whose name we know. When we see the dark powers being overcome, we know that nothing but the finger of God can be at work. In that case once again—and now in a radically new historic conjunction—we have to say that the Kingdom of God has come upon us.

6. Resistance and revolution

(a) Claiming our own lives: draft refusal

We press for renewal inside the Church because otherwise it will die, and we love what it stands for. We resist the State because if allowed to go unchecked it will do unforeseeable damage. Since the State is problematical, we can't ever be sure what effects our action will have on her. We therefore adopt a reasonable attack on a critical problem, without knowing what it will lead to. But in the community of love, we have full confidence that no honest work is without effect, even though we don't know where that effect will be.

Resistance to violence against the environment is largely symbolic—waiting for the day when a genuine police power will begin to clean up pollution. Resistance to violence against our psyche or tradition is the realm of spirituality and education; this is going on. Resistance to exploitation of the poor at home is an obvious critical duty. Each exploited class will take thought for itself, and we should ally ourselves with the clearest cases of need.

There remains resistance to exploitation abroad. Economic imperialism is elusive. It is no less dangerous on that account, but not quite so immediate a danger as the military imperialism which provides its sanction. The Viet Nam adventure has shown that hardware by itself is useless; only men will do.

The essence of Government policy is the ability to throw men in quickly where they're needed—perhaps in several countries at once. Quick call-up is impossible with a professional volunteer army, which must compete on the labor market. The Government realizes this. Therefore it's committed to keeping at least a token conscription in effect. This necessity is our opportunity. If many exemptions are granted, the injustice of the system becomes obvious. If many induction notices go out, the memory of Viet Nam will keep the resistance alive. The Government, much as it might like to, can't carry out its policies in complete independence of the citizen body.

Thus in any easily predictable future, the weak point of U.S. imperialist policy is the draft. In no predictable future is there any likelihood or danger of abolishing the U.S. military Establishment. The realistic goals are to make it harder for the United States to undertake counter-insurgency measures, and to create *some* area in our own society free of militarism, resuming control of our own lives. Thus the most constructive middle-term goal is mounting a campaign to destroy the Selective Service System.

The only alternative to a drafted army is a professional volunteer army at competitive salaries. This will bring its own dangers. It would be left without the leaven of good guys at tension with their own consciences. The police forces in our urban ghettos—a professional volunteer army of occupation—give us some idea what it would be like. But in fact those good guys aren't leavening it very much right now. We may gladly take up a new Administration's pledge to end the draft, which the generals must repudiate.

Denying the military an available manpower pool is the first step in altering neo-imperialist foreign policy. If by a big effort conscription were ended, the military would try to obtain the same results by improved weapons techniques and large-scale recruiting. The next realistic political task would be to put a ceiling on weapons development and recruitment: to deny money and men. Denying money calls for a campaign on the Congressional budget. Denying men would call for using student power and faculty power to break Government contracts with universities, and using resistance organization to convert men away from military careers and military engineering. These are long-term programs for limited goals. They'll be meaningful only as part of a constructive Quaker-style effort to work for peace and reconciliation.

It's very obvious that liberal Establishment organizations aren't going to mount the campaign against Selective Service. Our attack wouldn't have any spearhead if the Spirit had not already shown thousands of young men that cooperation with the draft was a denial of their manhood. (Here I rely on analyses by Bruce Nelson and Phil Farnham.) They're our moral leaders, and our beautifully simple course is to accept the clear-cut issue which History has made available. There's some possibility of redeeming the demonic State from its destructive course: by interposing our bodies. Whether we look at the needs of the planet, the Third World, our fellow-countrymen, our own souls—and all these are bound up in each other—the central moral issue of our time is limiting the State's power to do harm. Concretely, in the immediate future, this means *draft resistance*: aiding and abetting the young men who openly refuse cooperation with the Selective Service System.

Here is the precise point at which the Peace Movement is radicalizing the Church. There's no way the Church Establishment can encapsulate draft resistance, pretend that this is a project of its own devising. But neither, in view of the elegant parallel with the Church of the martyrs, can the hierarchies simply disavow draft resistance. This is the issue which forces the Established Church to say Yes and No *to itself.* For some time to come it will be the touchstone which will keep Christian radicals on the path of renewal and reunion—towards the global revolution in which, we now see, we're beginning to serve.

(b) The First World Revolution

The official story that America is a free democracy supporting free democracies is implemented in the streets. Our true political principles are being fulfilled by unexpected means in a second American revolution. And, since for the moment America stands on the growing edge of world history, we see also a turning point in colonialism. Our main institutional link to the Middle Ages and antiquity is the Church; and in the reshaping of our society, the Church is assuming a radically new form, suitable for export.

The conditions for these novelties were set (not to go further back) by the Industrial Revolution, which gave Western nations an internal and an external proletariat: the workers at home, and the colonial producers of raw materials and markets overseas. Exploitation of individuals and societies was accomplished by exploitation of nature. This factory imperialism provoked two reactions, which for a while it was able to co-opt. The Methodist revival and the missionary movement, at first opposed by the British Established Church, soon were seen as its best ally in keeping exploited populations content. Marx certainly regarded evangelical Christianity as an agent of capitalism, and in its place set proletarian revolution. In turn the scene of *its* biggest success takes the form of another imperialism, the Soviet, now putting down baby-steps to self-determination in Budapest, now in Prague.

But as exploitation of man and nature reaches the point of breakdown, there is a spontaneous rebellion, which humanizes and unifies the two earlier reactions. Socialist revolutions become smaller, more nationalistic, the work of a people living on its own land. A renewed Church reverts to the social conditions under which it was born. The convergence of Christianity and Marxism twists together two strands temporarily frayed from the same thread.

The worldwide Establishment has gotten together and set up

the United Nations as its house organ. America and Russia do their best to manage it in their joint interests. If it acquired more political power, it would solve some current problems and raise new ones. Neither it nor the Great Powers are any kind of guarantee against the exploitation of peoples. The United Nations is our best guarantee against violence towards the planetary environment, proliferation of people and bombs. We should support it for that purpose, but not expect it to do what it won't.

There's always some truth in it when a people takes a Messianic role on itself. Its government and propaganda are likely to play the part of antichrist; but somewhere inside it the right thing is to be found. The Roman Empire, Roman law, Vergil, distort but also transmit the reality expressed in the birth of Jesus. Anglo-American imperialism today is antichrist for much of the world; but the mythology of Milton and Blake, of the American frontier, point to a fulfillment still future. Our criticism of America can be so devastating precisely because her Messianic option is still open. Russian political Messianism has been more creative, and her novelists have expressed a radical Christian humanism more directly than in Europe.

Imperialism produced oppressed populations with common interests around the world. The two missionary faiths, Christianity and Marxism, organized the exploited peoples—once as imperial stooges, increasingly today in their own right. The people's revolution normally takes violent form for justice; where it's nonviolent, it's equivalent to the Church. There is indeed an international Socialist conspiracy: the bloc of liberation fronts with substantial justice on their side. I've sketched the beginnings of an underground ecumenical peace Church. Whatever their faults and compromises, we may say that *people's revolution and the people's Church are the political and spiritual organs of a renewed humanity.* At the right time of history, we see *the dawning outlines of global community organization against Establishment violence:* the First World Revolution.

For twenty centuries, the geographical spread of the Church, bringing paper reconciliation, has been accompanied by a progressive Establishment takeover, a collapse of resistance. Now the circle of the nations has been filled up; the first phase of the work is done. We're on the next upward sweep of the cycle and it's time for resistance to resume. As the political revolution sets up a Liberated Zone free of imperial control, the Church bears what the New Testament calls the "Kingdom of Heaven," and I translate as a transcendent Liberated Zone: an area in principle free from *all* exploitation. Both revolution and Church engage in resistance; but the Church's resistance cuts deeper, for it's turned also against the possibilities of exploitation in the revolution and in herself. The successive emergents of freedom and love have seeded the polis and the Church around the world. There's never yet been a form of the Church which was both apostolical and worldwide. But it's what we've been taught to expect by the New Testament, out of which (they say) there's fresh light yet to break. We see rising in the East what for the first time can properly be called *Church* history. The world is coming to a beginning.

Neither freedom nor love was an exclusive Western invention. There's no one figure which concentrates the discovery of freedom; but our tradition has held that the principle of love was concentrated in Jesus. The thing which he represents appears also in other traditions. Thomas Merton found Venerable Nhat Hanh—poet, ascetic, monk, lover of peace—far closer to himself than the bulk of his fellow Catholics were. If Jesus in fact represents the perfection of human nature, we'd expect that all peoples would have some intuition of the same excellence. As the Church spread across pagan Europe, it incorporated into its calendar a symbolic scheme of insights into the natural order. A pagan could have said that *his* religion had incorporated Jewish understanding of history into *its* pattern. A whole series of dialogues is called for with Buddhism, Judaism, Islam, Confucianism, in which we must trust that both sides will come out fulfilled. The precondition is that world Christianity should first regroup around the primitive Church. Constantine is losing and the radical Jesus is winning.

In the New Testament myth of the end of the world, as God does his new thing, there emerge new blessings and new woes, greater promises and threats than previously. This symbolism refers to our very own age, where the emergence of a worldwide re-

deemed humanity coexists with the threat of the world's end by
fire. Neither people's revolution nor people's Church has much
control over violence done by the demonically guided Great Powers of this age to the environment. At most the just revolutions can
help create a spirituality of family planning and piety towards nature—which would still have to be carried out through the United
Nations. But when war or fallout have done their worst, it's they
who'll be most acceptable to come in and start picking up the
pieces. Thus during the Viet Nam war, air traffic into Hanoi was
maintained by an International Control Commission staffed by representative weaker nations: India, Poland, Canada. And the Americans who went in and out on it were Quakers, pacifists, blacks,
students, professors, women, revolutionaries.

When a family moves into a new city, they live out of suitcases
and snap at each other until they put their house and garden in
order and settle in. Only then can they begin some constructive
vocation and family life. The human race has reached this point
only in peaceful enclaves like Scandinavia and Canada—both noted
for forest management. Ahead lie endless possibilities of guiding
planetary evolution and our numbers. Only then will we be able
to open up the luggage we've brought along—languages, science,
the arts, space travel—and for the first time find out its use. I have
a dream that the tormented shores of southeast Asia, South Africa
—every seabeach in its summer—have become a second Mediterranean splashing with comely brown bodies, while temples of a
thousand architectures rise from each city on its hill.

The threads of cable, roads, radio, airlines binding the planet
together—still mostly for propaganda or manipulation—are the
filaments of a self-spun cocoon. As it matures, we see a series of
unrelated changes in what still looks like a caterpillar. But at God's
right time, the slender thorax, the antennae, the unexpanded wings
take on an organic unity, and it's the stiffening cast of the chrysalis
which is seen as the anomaly. We haven't got any way of telling
what form the demonic forces of exploitation will next take. But
we can say that for the first time the radical unity of the human
race in love, the immortal butterfly of Earth, is free to take wing
as soon as it's passionately affirmed.

(c) Life in the Liberated Zone

The Liberated Zone is brought into existence through our action in history. But in a way hard to describe we're contemporaries of all who've realized it in the past; and by anticipation we share the perfection it's moving toward. A tourist guide to that country would be the most valuable thing we could lay our hands on.

As soon as we say that, we realize we've all along had it in our possession.

Still it needs to be adapted for the people of different backgrounds who'll be taking up residence there. The present manual only sketches the principal international means of travel to the Liberated Zone; gives a few practical hints about luggage, clothing, and health precautions; notes the customs formalities; and includes a brief historical sketch. I can see that a handbook of quite different content is required for those planning an extended stay. Actually every long-term resident is his own best source for local customs. But I've taken the liberty of setting down some general observations, which I hope to publish elsewhere before too long. In particular I'll try to suggest helpful lines of conduct for persons involved in border incidents—still more frequent than we could wish. Perhaps any readers who've found the present volume useful will also want to be on the lookout for its successor; even though the author's claim rests less on any encyclopedic knowledge of the country, than on simple admiration for the character of the inhabitants, the traditions of their national life, and the charm of the unspoiled landscape.